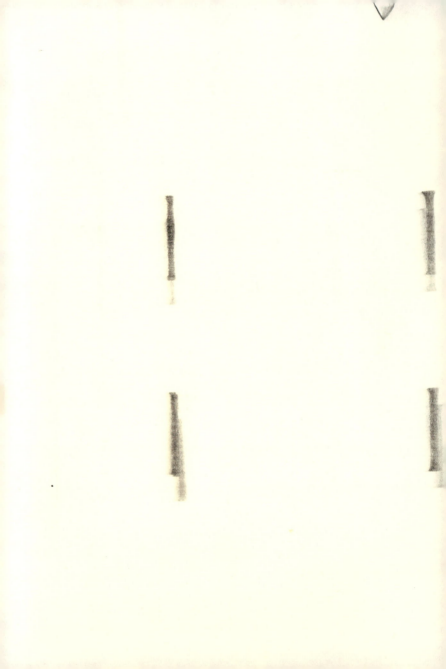

UNDERSTANDING
JOHN BARTH

Understanding Contemporary American Literature

Matthew J. Bruccoli, *Editor*

UNDERSTANDING
John
BARTH

by STAN FOGEL
and GORDON SLETHAUG

91279

UNIVERSITY OF SOUTH CAROLINA PRESS

Published in Columbia, South Carolina, by the
University of South Carolina Press

Manufactured in the United States of America

First Edition

Library of Congress Cataloguing-in-Publication Data

Fogel, Stanley.
    Understanding John Barth / by Stan Fogel and Gordon Slethaug.
1st ed.
        p.   cm. — (Understanding contemporary American literature)
    Includes bibliographical references.
        ISBN 0–87249–660–0
        1. Barth, John—Criticism and interpretation. I. Slethaug,
    Gordon. II. Series.
    PS3552.A75Z625   1990
    813'.54—dc20   90–11937
                                                        CIP

From S. F. to J. J. Ink
From G. S. to Darin, Gavin, and Kris

CONTENTS

EDITOR'S PREFACE

Understanding Contemporary American Literature has been planned as a series of guides or companions for students as well as good nonacademic readers. The editor and publisher perceive a need for these volumes because much of the influential contemporary literature makes special demands. Uninitiated readers encounter difficulty in approaching works that depart from the traditional forms and techniques of prose and poetry. Literature relies on conventions, but the conventions keep evolving; new writers form their own conventions—which in time may become familiar. Put simply, *UCAL* provides instruction in how to read certain contemporary writers—identifying and explicating their material, themes, use of language, point of view, structures, symbolism, and responses to experience.

The word *understanding* in the series title was deliberately chosen. Many willing readers lack an adequate understanding of how contemporary literature works; that is, what the author is attempting to express and the means by which it is conveyed. Although the criticism and analysis in the series have been aimed at a level of general accessibility, these introductory volumes are meant to be applied in conjunction with the works they cover. Thus they do not provide a substitute for the works and authors they introduce, but rather prepare the reader for more profitable literary experiences.

M. J. B.

ACKNOWLEDGMENTS

Thanks to Rita Racanelli for her care with the manuscript and to Sophie Thomas for her help with the bibliography.

UNDERSTANDING
JOHN BARTH

CHAPTER ONE

Understanding John Barth

Career

John Barth (along with John Hawkes, Thomas Pynchon, William Gass, Robert Coover, and Donald Barthelme) is responsible for the redefinition of fiction in America that has taken place in the last twenty-five years. He has helped to give fiction a theoretical turn, steering it away from the conventionally realistic use of plot and character, from an emphasis on verisimilitude or the texture of daily life, toward a concern with the writing of fiction itself.

The most optimistic of this group of writers, who, with the exception of Barthelme who died in 1989, in the late 1980s are in their late fifties or early sixties, Barth was born on May 27, 1930, in the small town of Cambridge, Maryland, the seat of Dorchester County. All of the novels, especially the two most recent, *Sabbatical* and *The Tidewater Tales*, are saturated with the Maryland-Baltimore locale and include details of crabbing and sailing as well as elements of the region's history.

UNDERSTANDING JOHN BARTH

With his twin sister, Jill, Barth began school in a system he called unaffluent, semirural, and semi-Southern. Until he was steered into an academic program and she into a commercial option, they were inseparable and referred to as Jack and Jill. After completing Cambridge High School, Barth briefly studied in 1947 at the Juilliard School of Music in New York City. An avid player of jazz and the drums, Barth, nevertheless, began to doubt his own musical talents and grew concerned about the Juilliard's steep tuition, so he accepted a scholarship from The Johns Hopkins University, from which he graduated in 1951 with a B.A. in creative writing. He then continued into the M.A. program, in which, as part of his academic requirements, he wrote a novel, "Shirt of Nessus," which was never published. Barth completed his M.A. in 1952 and began to study for the Ph.D. With increasing family responsibilities—in 1950 he married Harriette Anne Strickland who gave birth to Christine in 1951 and John in 1952 and they expected the birth of another (Daniel) in 1954—he took a job in English composition at the Pennsylvania State University in 1953. After a stint as an instructor there, he moved in 1965 to the State University of New York at Buffalo. In 1969, after four years in Buffalo together, he and his wife divorced. In late 1970 he married a former student, Shelly Rosenberg. In 1973 Barth returned with his second wife to the Baltimore area where, alternating between his city home and a summer home on the Eastern Shore, he continues to teach in the Writing Seminars

CAREER

program at The Johns Hopkins University and, when he can, sails the Chesapeake.

The integration of academic and literary careers is a significant dimension of Barth's work. He has spent a great deal of time lecturing on, as well as writing, novels; in addition, he incorporates passages into his fiction exploring how to write and presents a rationale for why he does what he does. The tendency to examine the nature of fiction gives Barth's texts the self-conscious, philosophizing character that has become a distinctive practice among current writers.

Barth's first two novels, *The Floating Opera* (1956) and *The End of the Road* (1958), are basically realistic— less wordy, less complex, and less radical structurally than the works that follow. Nonetheless, despite the ease with which they can be read as realistic fictions, their preoccupation with suicide and nihilism is rendered in an ironic way, one that provides the realization that this, indeed, is the end of the road for the linear, action-oriented novel.

The next two novels, *The Sot-Weed Factor* and *Giles Goat-Boy*, were published in 1960 and 1966 and also can be seen to form a pair. (Twinning, as Barth points out in one of the essays in *The Friday Book*, is important to his literary as well as his family life.) Both are long, sprawling novels in which parody comes to the fore as a dominant device. In *The Sot-Weed Factor* Barth undermines many sacred dimensions of American history and the American character. *Giles Goat-Boy* contains a compendium of parodies on important aspects of the cultural and religious fabric of Western civilization such as the Bible, *Oedipus Rex*, and American-Russian relations.

Lost in the Funhouse (1968), published a year after Barth's famous essay "The Literature of Exhaustion" appeared in *The Atlantic Monthly*, engages the means of fiction almost at the expense of content. His most concentrated play with, as well as exploration of, the verities of fiction (plot, character, theme, and setting) stems from questions raised in "The Literature of Exhaustion" about how to write in an era which differs markedly from previous ones.

Chimera (1972) is a sustained deployment of and assault on mythology, one of Barth's favorite targets and also one of his favorite subjects. Composed of three novellas, *Chimera* retells the story of Scheherazade in *The Thousand and One Nights* as well as the Greek myths of Perseus and Bellerophon. Barth's fiction, like Barthelme's and Coover's, shows a suspicion of, and fascination with, those enduring or ahistorical stories celebrated by Joyce and Lawrence as compensation for the loss of religious faith. After having had two of his earlier works nominated for a National Book Award, Barth won the Award in 1973 for *Chimera*.

In 1979 Barth's longest and most demanding work, *LETTERS*, appeared. It features characters from his earlier published works as well as Germaine Pitt, Lady Amherst, a British academic and literary woman. These characters exchange letters with each other and with

CAREER

"John Barth, Author." Thus, Barth offers the readers sequels to the earlier books, as well as a self-contained novel.

The two most recent novels, *Sabbatical: A Romance* (1983) and *The Tidewater Tales: A Novel* (1987), provide a glimpse of the more extended, less convoluted narrative style of which Barth, a lover of stories and storytelling, is capable. They also reveal a Barth more committed to social and political issues than in previous books. *Sabbatical: A Romance* features a couple named Fenwick Turner and Susan Seckler, who sail from Chesapeake Bay to the Caribbean and back. They speculate in a leisurely way about literature and in a more anxious way about, among other things, the CIA. *The Tidewater Tales: A Novel* can be understood as a companion piece to *Sabbatical* or on its own. The two main characters, Peter and Katherine Sherritt Sagamore, sail on Chesapeake Bay in their boat *Story*, telling stories.

Many of Barth's essays have also appeared in a collection called *The Friday Book.* They explicitly reveal what the novels imply: a love of what fiction is made of and how it is made. As Barth writes in *Chimera, "the key to the treasure is the treasure."*[1] Reveling in and examining fiction, Barth shows no signs of flagging energy; he is a prolific writer whose oeuvre will no doubt continue to expand. Barth has received a good many honors, among them an honorary Litt.D., from the University of Maryland in 1969, and grants from the Rockefeller Foundation in 1965 and the American Academy in 1966. He

UNDERSTANDING JOHN BARTH

was named to the American Academy of Arts and Sciences in 1977. Revealingly, Barth's personal life and academic awards are less important to his fiction than the engagement with theory that marks his life as a writer. In considering Barth, biographical detail can be subordinated to issues of literature and criticism.

Overview

LETTERS, Giles Goat-Boy, The Sot-Weed Factor, and *The Tidewater Tales* average around eight hundred pages; they need only be lifted to convey the sense that here are some daunting works. If the mere weight were not enough, the books' false forewords and appendixes, complex tables of contents, academic charts and diagrams, and characters moving from book to book demonstrate that a compact synthesis of Barth's ideas and techniques would not only be impossible to provide, but would also reduce the richness and energy of the volumes.

Along with Pynchon's *Gravity's Rainbow*, Coover's *The Public Burning*, and William Gaddis' *The Recognitions*, Barth's massive and sprawling works are part luxuriant, meandering narratives, part circuitous, dense, labyrinthine mazes. One characteristic of postmodern American fiction is the refusal on the part of writers to accommodate themselves to mainstream tastes. Because many of Barth's works are long, some readers balk at the sheer

OVERVIEW

length of these volumes, although they are rich and absorbing, and prefer the more concise Barth of *The Floating Opera, Sabbatical,* and especially, *Lost in the Funhouse.* In the last-named work, one story, printed on the outside margin of the first page, simply reads, "Once upon a time/there was a story that began."[2] Cut out, twisted once, and attached end to end, the strip of paper links the two phrases, producing an infinitely long story that encompasses and mirrors all the stories of people's individual, cultural, and historical lives. Barth's projects are thus dual: To create the extended and expansive novel that weaves tales and to invent the short piece of fiction that scrutinizes storytelling. Barth often compresses these elements into one work.

To understand contemporary American literature, generally, and Barth, specifically, is to come to grips with a good deal of experimentation in tale-telling and theorizing about telling. Those writers who engage in this double writing can be called postmodern. In an interview with Joe David Bellamy, Barth divides writers into traditional and experimental or postmodern camps. Saul Bellow, John Updike, and Joseph Heller are considered traditional; Gass, Hawkes, and Barthelme are deemed experimental. Writers in both groups are contemporary; that is to say, they write in the period after World War II. Bellow, Updike, and Heller are seen by Barth as the inheritors of the modernist tradition, profoundly influenced by a feeling of discontinuity between the literature, spiritual tradition, and social mores of

previous periods and that of the twentieth century. Typi-
fying modernism is a sense of loss of order, coherence,
and meaning in the increasingly urban world. Both World
War I and World War II radically changed the shape of
European and American cultures and effectively dispos-
sessed modern men and women of their belief in a
universe laden with absolute values, God, tradition, reason, and individual intuition. Modernist writers are concerned with the disintegration of the modern society
and the disappearance of a unified view of the self; for
Barth they tend to express these anxieties in ways that
affirm the novel's ability to tell truths. Barth, however,
clearly sympathizes and identifies with the experimen-
talists, those who reject and/or handle self-consciously
the traditional staples of the novel. (Hawkes's maxim
that the true enemies of the novel are plot, character,
theme, and setting applies here.) Thus, in one of his
typically extended novels, *The Sot-Weed Factor*, Barth in-
dulges and luxuriates in extravagant, protracted stories
about the founding of America that might be more typically associated with an eighteenth-century novelist; at
the same time, he draws attention to the artifice of the
storyteller's art.

As he writes in an essay, "The Literature of Replenishment," the "true postmodernist . . . keeps one foot
always in the narrative past . . . and one foot in, one
might say, the Parisian structuralist present."[3] That present is a highly self-reflexive space in which realism, a
"good read" without an ongoing awareness of the

OVERVIEW

conventions of fiction, is no longer allowed or offered. (Parisian structuralists, for Barth, are those—for example, Roland Barthes and Jacques Derrida—who have been prominent in emphasizing the act of reading rather than the content of reading.) Therefore, understanding Barth requires understanding this paradox: He loves the myths, stories, and techniques that saturate accessible, realistic works of fiction, yet he cannot merely retell or re-present them. The Bible, stories about early America, *The Odyssey*, folktales, the epistolary novel popularized by Samuel Richardson in *Clarissa*—Barth uses these materials and forms, but he does not employ them traditionally. He is too aware of their formulaic, stylized qualities; "there's no going back to Tolstoy and Dickens" except on nostalgia trips[4] (which Barth frequently takes, all the while drawing the reader's attention to the fact that he is on a nostalgia trip and that he knows he is on it).

Like many postmodern writers, Barth is leery of the way a reader will try to fit his works into orthodox categories. Again a paradox is at work here: Barth loves to tell stories to rapt audiences, action often giving way in Barth's works to the relating of a story that generates another story that generates. . . . An appropriate image for this activity of Barth's is the thousand-and-one stories of the Arabian nights in which Scheherazade must string story after story together to save her life; if she offends her listener, she forfeits her life. (Scheherazade and her story play an important role in *Chimera*.) However, despite his love of storytelling, Barth also teases and chides his audience for responding to those very stories: "The reader! You dogged, uninsultable, print-oriented bastard, it's you I'm addressing, who else, from inside this monstrous fiction. You've read me this far, then? Even this far? For what discreditable motive? How is it you don't go to a movie, watch TV . . . ?"[5]

Behind this jesting lies an insecurity about the way many readers might want to appropriate fiction; their voyeuristic desires for scenes and events, their impatience with demands placed upon them in the reading of unconventional literature could be undercutting a work's vitality and uniqueness. This unease, for instance, propelled Vladimir Nabokov to write a "Foreword" to *Lolita* in which he ironically urges readers to identify with the characters and to digest the novel as a potboiler or a cautionary tale. His false encouragement draws attention to the ways that readers tend to accept the language of fiction as realistic and literal. Reading against the grain, that is, halting and changing seemingly spontaneous habits of reading and understanding a text, is a more conscious, scrutinizing process in which the naturalness of language is devalued and its materiality (its physical properties) is recognized. This is what Barth advocates. Reading against the grain makes for the kind of story or novel that both advances and retreats, that draws the readers in, then cauterizes their intuitive, habitual response.

It is worth contending with this notion for a little

OVERVIEW

longer because reading against the grain is not the trained or reflexive response to fiction of most North American readers, and the willingness to engage in such a practice will mark the success and pleasure gained from one of Barth's (or Barthelme's or Walter Abish's or Kathy Acker's) works. Indeed, Barth offers tantalizing ways of coming to terms with and developing such a reading technique. Pynchon's *Gravity's Rainbow* and Barthelme's *Snow White* confront the reader with disruption or excess. In the latter book the typeface is often altered; the style shifts from stream of consciousness to pop-rock lyrics to academic jargon. In the former the vocabulary is difficult, the plot is monumentally and dauntingly confused and confusing, and the novel's scope defies a concise overview. In short, these novels force reading against the grain, violating and denying expectations regarding fiction at every turn.

Lost in the Funhouse is Barth's testament to this kind of postmodern demand. Otherwise, his fiction contains "both/and" paradigms: both reveling in storytelling and dislocation of that storytelling, both rich, leisurely narration and terse, caustic denial of narration, and both theory and fiction. In Barth's own metaphor, one wants in a lover both heartfelt desire and technical virtuosity or skill—having the first alone provides ineptness, the second alone coldness. In other words, meshing the extremes produces a richer, more balanced performance. Thus, Barth's fiction is probably the best introduction to the experimentation and playfulness of postmodernism. Barthelme's parody, Pynchon's complexity, and Coover's energy are all apparent in Barth's oeuvre, along with a comfortable quality, and a love of (yet skepticism about) narration that make his work approachable. In an era emphasizing rigorous and uncompromising engagement with the dimensions of fiction, Barth's warmth is a captivating quality. In short, his paradoxes and disruptions are not estranging.

In *Snow White* Barthelme writes that one of his character's favorite forms is the palinode. The palinode is, quite simply, a formal retraction. It involves recanting something that was said or written previously and permits art without affirmation, an important dimension of postmodern fiction. Julio Cortázar in *Hopscotch*, for instance, provides a chapter grid in a prefatory note that allows the readers the possibility of two readings of the same novel, one a linear one, the other a "hopscotching" one that moves from a chapter in the middle of the text to one near the end to one near the beginning and so forth. The second reading undoes the plot developed in the first, producing retraction, art without affirmation. In other words, the postmodern writer wishes to write something without wanting to emphasize or value some *thing*. To ask what Barth is for, the way one asks what Lawrence is for (paganism, myth)or Woolf is for (stoicism, art), is to miss his palinodic art. Some of Barth's experiments with palinodes are quite complex.

In *Giles Goat-Boy* Barth tells traditional Biblical stories (of Moses, of the Sermon on the Mount) in such a way that Giles is both Moses and Jesus; however, the notion of hero or savior is rendered dubiously, skeptically. Modern (as opposed to postmodern) literature might be said to be mythopoeic, affirming myth. T. S. Eliot in "The Waste Land" (1922) celebrates those cultures (ancient Greece, Renaissance England) that he felt shared the same stories of creation, the same moral code, as well as a sense of absolute values. Similarly, Northrop Frye, who might be called the literary critic of modernism, seeks (and discovers) Western myth as the common element in the literature of all periods. Unlike Eliot and Frye, Barth and the other postmodernists are dubious about such a generalization, such a broad schema. To unite all literatures via myth is to overvalue one specific set of stories or one specific pattern. Thus, Barth weaves myths into his novels and short stories in order to perform his palinodic tricks, to reveal the stylized, fictive, relativistic dimensions of mythology.

Positivism, the idea that there is some thing to express, gets scrutinized and diminished by Barth. He accepts the contrary notion that life is secondary to language. Instead of writing as if language is a window onto the world, Barth writes as if language and life have a much more mixed relationship. One of the major reasons that postmodern writers of fiction and criticism disrupt the normative reader's expectations is that they cannot affirm language as a transparent medium that allows them to use it to present a scene or idea or emotion neutrally. For them language is the central property out of which reality and life are made. Its conventions and dimensions are the most important element in the construction of reality. If all conceptualizing is fiction-making, as Coover has pointed out, the role of the novelist differs vastly from that of passive observer, assessor of reality, or receiver of divine truths. Barth seizes on this altered sense of the relationship of words and world to construct and present an altered sense of fiction. That this divergent way of writing is perhaps no longer as eccentric to a reader in the late 1980s as it may have been earlier is due in part to Barth's groundbreaking departures from orthodoxy.

Barth asks that his readers take to his avant-garde pieces the following: a different set of expectations, a recognition that habitual ways of writing are not sacred or inviolable, and a skepticism regarding traditional texts as models. These traits have come to be called decon-structive—taking apart the structures, patterns, and expectations of text, context, author, and reader. Although Barth's critical work, collected in *The Friday Book*, does not have the tortuous academic qualities that mark contemporary critical theories, his affinities with deconstruction are strong. Deconstruction loosens meanings (rather than fixing them), casts into doubt the systems that enshrine established texts as classics, and regards language as a labyrinth of words (rather than an instrument of truth telling). It can be understood as a vital postmodern critical practice akin to the experimentation and focuses of Barth's literary practice. His fiction itself contains numerous passages that could be found in scholarly journals dealing with criticism and literature. There are copious amounts of theoretical material in, for example, *Lost in the Funhouse* with its "Freitag's Triangle," a schematic representation of development in narrative; in the fictive editorial opinions rendered in a coda to *Giles Goat-Boy*; in examination of the nature and taxonomies (or systems of classification) of myth in *Chimera*.

Deconstruction's suspicion of the intellectual and philosophical systems that enclose people, providing the contexts within which they think and act; its love of multiple and contrary meanings of words and texts—these qualities Barth adopts to produce his fictions. Barth's detractors, in fact, sound like deconstruction's detractors: they resent books that are playful and dispersive, rather than serious and integrative. The most hostile critic, perhaps, was John Gardner whose *On Moral Fiction* Barth has called "an exercise in literary kneecapping that lumps modernists and postmodernists together without distinction and consigns us all to Hell with the indiscriminate fervor characteristic of late converts to the right."[6] Gardner contended that Barth and his kind reject plots and characters, thereby turning their backs on the moral aspect of fiction. What he did not understand is that every technique involves choices, that novels that draw attention to their formal or technical elements convey moral nuances as surely and as tellingly as those that deal with moral issues in seemingly more direct ways. Mary McCarthy is another who finds much to complain about in Barth's fiction, stating that she prefers writers such as Philip Roth and Bernard Malamud, who look critically at society from the point of view of the ethnic outsider and make demands on their readers only by the moral and ethical dilemmas of their characters, but who do not tamper with traditional approaches to novel writing. For McCarthy, Barth is too academic, too university-oriented. In addition, she derides the intellectual milieu that champions Barth and complains about the "reviewers and teachers of literature, who, as always, are the reader's main foe."[7]

The postmodern novel, it is true, with its palinodic focus and attempt to force a reading against the grain, does require more of the reader than the traditional novel. It is also true that Barth and a number of others rebuked by McCarthy do teach in universities and spend time exploring and discussing the theory of fiction. This academic centeredness can lead to the charge of elitism. Certainly, Barth's use of parody requires knowledge of that which is being parodied (myth in *Giles Goat-Boy*, the historical novel in *The Sot-Weed Factor*, the epistolary novel in *LETTERS*, the sea voyage in *Sabbatical* and *The Tidewater Tales*) for the desired effect to be achieved. In addition, parody can be used to draw attention to and disrupt what have been thought of as natural reading practices; thus, comfortable and habitual ways of absorbing large passages can be blocked. Most of Barth's targets, though, as large as they are, can be recognized by anyone who has read such works as the Bible, histories of America, or realistic fiction.

In the main, Barth's work can be read *with,* as well as against, the grain. Once tutored in and alert to Barth's parody, the reader can appreciate incrementally the devices at work. As defined by Linda Hutcheon in *A Theory of Parody*, parody is one of the "techniques of self-referentiality by which art reveals its awareness of the context/dependent nature of meaning."[8] That is, parody draws attention to the conventions used in fiction, even realistic fiction, which is not a neutral medium. Parody can be seen as one of the many anti-realist devices that serve to sharpen the readers' awareness of what they are reading. Active readers will find pleasure in Barth's parodies of the major forms and stories of Western culture not only because Barth recycles these interestingly, but also because the readers can go back to the originals with a heightened sense of their context, their specificity.

It is hard to accept rejections of Barth's work by critics who, themselves, are, for the most part, readers who take risks. Leslie Fiedler, for instance, summarizes his engagement with one of Barth's longer works this way: "I have tried recently, with some difficulty, to read my way through John Barth's *LETTERS.*"[9] Fiedler, who was a colleague of Barth's at SUNY-Buffalo, also maintains that while countless students in the early 1970s chorused that *Jonathan Livingston Seagull* changed their lives, nary a one was overheard to say that *Lost in the Funhouse* stimulated him or her in like manner.

Lost in the Funhouse contains elements frequently found in literature—heroism, boyhood outings, competition for a partner. It, however, scrutinizes such plots and the literary presentation of them. The heroism story, "Night-Sea Journey," is a parody of a quest in which spermatozoa swim indomitably towards a possible rendezvous with a waiting-to-be-fertilized egg. The boyhood outing, "Lost in the Funhouse," combines nascent sexual longings with discussions of plot lines, and climaxes. "Petition," the story that tells of the competition for a woman, involves Siamese twins joined in a way meant to parallel and parody the mind-body duality philosophers and theologians (as well as novelists) often accept. Read as literal or realistic pieces, they seem silly; reread (in a postmodern way), they provide a witty, pithy sense of the way stories are told and of the way political, theological, and philosophical stories get passed off as truths. They also are engrossing, keeping one guessing about the success of the spermatozoa or the plight of the soul and body. Nonetheless, these stories would be inane if suspense were the sole end. Barth's interest lies in the ways writers manufacture suspense and, indeed, narrative; it also lies in the exploration and reduction of concepts such as heroism and the mind-body duality. Realism is regarded suspiciously as the unwitting ally of believable, solidified terms, shoring them up, lending them authenticity. For John Sturrock,

OVERVIEW

realism "makes . . . literature the servant of reality because it holds the instrumental view of language," suggesting "that 'through' words we look at life."[10]

Returning to Fiedler's complaint one realizes that it is not merely wrong; it also affirms a too simplistic, too positivistic way of reading the world. In the same essay Fiedler states, rather perplexingly, that he yearns for those glorious days of the eighteenth and nineteenth centuries during which a work such as Samuel Richardson's *Clarissa* and works by Fyodor Dostoevski and Leo Tolstoy could be read "with equal pleasure in the kitchen, the parlor, the nursery."[11] Richardson's novel and his period may seem more accessible because they have been examined extensively; they have become, or are thought to be, "known." Ironically, Barth's novel, because it and his period are still fresh, is more taxing. Fiedler seems not to realize that a novel of one thousand or so pages will, no doubt, always be formidable and daunting, whether it was written two hundred or two years ago. But one who has seen a play written by Samuel Beckett, viewed a movie directed by Jean-Luc Goddard, or read a poem written by John Ashbery should not be utterly befuddled by a novelist whose long work disrupts plot sequences or character development or description. Or in William Gass's wonderful metaphor that links lovemaking and reading, "Only a literalist at loving would expect to plug ahead like the highway people's line machine, straight over hill and dale. . . ."[12]

The coupling of lovemaking and reading suggests

the playfulness of postmodern fiction. Like Giles, the nascent Grand Tutor of *Giles Goat-Boy*, Barth apprehends the unreality, the fictiveness of the so-called real world. To quote Giles: "Indeed, if I never came truly to despair at the awful arbitrariness of facts, it was because I never more than notionally accepted them. The *Encyclopedia Tammanica* I read from Aardvaark to Zymurgy in quite the same spirit as I read the *Old School Tales*, my fancy prefacing each entry 'Once upon a time. . . .'"[13] Once upon a time, reality was that from which fiction was derived and play was similarly subordinated to the seemingly more substantial real world. For Barth, as well as other postmodern writers of theory and fiction, the relationships are, as disruptive as it sounds, reversed. The gambit of repeating the phrase, "Once upon a time," is one with which Barth himself would be sympathetic. At a key moment in *Giles Goat-Boy*, a chase scene in which George hunts Bray, a librarian is hurriedly asked whether she has seen someone pass by; she looks up from a book she is reading which contains the very passage in which she is a player. Tactics such as that force the readers' focus away from content and realism, towards the language of the novel and conventions of fiction. Reading innocently or naively becomes impossible.

That fiction precedes reality is an uncommon notion; that play precedes and shapes reality—and that realism is something that blinds one to this process—is an even more radical view. Indeed, because of the trivi-

OVERVIEW

alizing connotations of the word *playful,* a better word to define the tendency is *ludic,* from the Latin word *ludere* (to play). The ludic sensibility tends to see the structures that lie behind and determine reality and seeks to discover and expose the rules of the various games people play. The premise here is that all of the social, psychological, economic, historical, and literary dimensions of reality can be appropriated to a games model, to a series of codes that can be read or studied, if not solved. For Gass, for instance, philosophy and fiction can both be understood as games, similar ones at that, with the latter providing the principal activity: "They are divine games. Both play at gods as others play at bowls; for there is frequently more reality in fairy tales than in these magical constructions of the mind. . . ."[14] For Gass philosophers differ from writers of fiction only in that the former have been telling lies for a longer time than novelists (whose craft, it is said, is only two hundred or so years old); Gass adds that the soul is an invention much as a literary character is.

One of the clichés that gets bandied about regarding novels by Barth is that they are pessimistic and that they herald the death of the novel. Charles Molesworth, typical of many, has written, "To choose between, say, John Barth and S. Beckett, might be to choose between two exhaustions, two forms of fully articulated 'belatedness.' As we used to say back home, 'mighty slim pickins,' indeed."[15] That *Giles Goat-Boy, The Sot-Weed Factor, LETTERS,* or *The Tidewater Tales* can be regarded as betraying exhaustion should perplex anyone who has read them. They are, in fact, long and intricate but, above all, energetic. George Giles quests avidly; Burlingame eats avidly; Germaine and Ambrose copulate avidly; Peter and Katherine Sagamore tell stories avidly. Barth, it can be assumed, writes avidly, and devotees of Barth's fiction, evidently, read avidly. That Barth regards philosophical and social constructs as models, hypotheses, fictions, does not mean that he does not derive a good deal of pleasure from them. Probably the most pronounced error in the understanding of postmodern fiction occurs in the assessment of the spirit in which it is produced. Too often critics think of Barth and other postmodernists as nihilistic, reduced to the status of Hamm and Clov in Beckett's *Endgame*, contemplating a fragmented and chaotic world. Nothing could be further from the truth; rather, they glory in a world that is malleable, a world in which fiction is the central property. Barth's most famous dictum in this regard is that God wasn't a bad novelist, but he was a realist. What passes for truth in the mundane, middle-class world is a legislated normality, one that can be altered—and fiction is the medium for change.

UNDERSTANDING JOHN BARTH

Notes

1. John Barth, *Chimera* (New York: Random House, 1972) 11.

2. John Barth, *Lost in the Funhouse: Fiction for Print, Tape, Live Voice* (Garden City, N.Y.: Doubleday, 1968) 1–2.

3. John Barth, "The Literature of Replenishment: Postmodernist Fiction," *The Friday Book: Essays and Other Nonfiction* (New York: Putnam, 1984) 204.

4. Barth, "The Literature of Replenishment" 202.

5. Barth, *Lost in the Funhouse* 127.

6. Barth, "The Literature of Replenishment" 196–97.

7. Mary McCarthy, *Ideas and the Novel* (New York: Harcourt Brace Jovanovich, 1980) 121.

8. Linda Hutcheon, *A Theory of Parody: The Teachings of Twentieth Century Art Forms* (New York: Methuen, 1985) 85.

9. Leslie Fiedler, "The Death and Rebirth of the Novel," *Salmagundi* 50–51 (1980–81): 144.

10. John Sturrock, "Roland Barthes," *Structuralism and Since*, ed. John Sturrock (Oxford: Oxford University Press, 1979) 65.

11. Fiedler 145.

12. William Gass, *Willie Master's Lonesome Wife* (New York: Knopf, 1971) no pagination.

13. John Barth, *Giles Goat-Boy* (New York: Doubleday, 1966) 81.

14. Gass, *Fiction and the Figures of Life* (New York: Knopf, 1970) 4.

15. Charles Molesworth, "Reflections," *Salmagundi* 50–51 (1980–81): 103.

CHAPTER TWO

The Floating Opera

Although John Barth began by writing short stories, his career was officially launched with the publication of his first two novels, *The Floating Opera* and *The End of the Road*. Written in the first part of 1955, *The Floating Opera* was quickly followed by *The End of the Road*, completed in the last three months of 1955. The first was published in 1956 and the second in 1958. Unhappy with the first edition of *The Floating Opera* because the publisher insisted on structural and tonal alterations, Barth published a revised edition in 1967, which restored his original design.

Most characters and events are common to both editions. The narrator, Todd Andrews, who is a lawyer, searches through self-inquiry to find personal meaning within a perplexing and alienating universe. Having fought in World War I and survived its atrocities, Todd grasps his own brutality but fails to comprehend the suicide of his father. These facts of existence, along with a heart condition, interfere with his relationships, so that his liaison with the wealthy, sophisticated Jane Mack

THE FLOATING OPERA

and his friendship with her husband, Harrison, are governed by his physical weakness and negative opinion of human nature. Even his relationship with Jeannine Mack, possibly his daughter, cannot free him of such negativity.

Todd's guarded but changing relationships with other acquaintances—his secretary Mrs. Lake, his client Dorothy Miner, his partner Mr. Bishop, his fellow boarders at the hotel (Captain Osborn Jones and Mister Haecker), and his doctor Marvin Rose—are governed by deception, subterfuge, and mistrust. His inability to communicate with others and failed attempt at suicide on board the showboat, *Floating Opera,* must be seen against the backdrop of irrationality, brutality, war, and death. In *The Floating Opera* Barth explores the ideas that people hold, their perceptions, and statements about themselves. Those subjects that he investigates include the tension between the urge to live and the desire to die, between what human beings want to be and what they are, between subconscious sexual drives and conscious rational processes, between human violence and elaborate systems of justice, and between events and attribution of causes.

Both the first and second editions treat Todd Andrews' reactions to a central paradox—that, despite overwhelming reasons to accept, and even seek, death, most people aspire to continue living. To come to terms with this enigma, he explores an opposite case, his own father's suicide; but, finding no answer, he decides to commit suicide, himself. That event is accidentally interrupted, and he consequently finds no more reason to die than to live. In the process of reaching this conclusion he discovers that intentionality and reason provide no understanding of, and little basis for, human activity, and that chance and accident continually alter behavior. The interrupted seduction of Betty June, the quixotic killing of the German soldier in the Argonne Forest, and the onset of his affair with Jane Mack—all are unintentioned and unmotivated, yet each fundamentally affects the way he perceives himself and the world. Both editions alternate between a comic and a despairing vision of man's irrationality and animality.

The first and second editions diverge about midpoint in the novel. In chapter 11 of the second edition Todd refers to the ironic conjunction of copulating dogs, which block a funeral procession, whereas in the first edition the irony hinges on a pregnant cat blocking the procession. As Enoch Jordan remarks, this comic image of the copulating dogs makes Todd's animality more intense in the second edition.[1] In chapter 12 the amusement of the old men watching the copulating dogs prepares for comments in chapter 13 about Todd's failed seduction of Betty June and her subsequent hatred for him, which is so great that she tries to kill him in chapter 14.

This second edition, which deletes chapter 23 ("Another Premise to Swallow") and rearranges other episodes, is less sentimental and better organized than the

first—generally leaner and less self-indulgent. The omitted chapter is one that restates in didactic form the general drift of the dramatic dialogue between Todd and
Jeannine in chapter 22, concerning the failure of reason
to answer the hard questions of existence. The thrust
of the content in the final chapters has also been altered.
The first edition's final three chapters become four. Information is added about Todd's attempt to blow up the
entire boat while committing suicide and his lack of concern that he has callously endangered the lives of those
he cares about—Jane and Jeannine, Mr. Bishop, Marvin
Rose, and Captain Osborn. This changes the tone of the
final scene when Todd and Captain Osborn leave the
boat and coolly chat a moment with the Macks, whom
Todd has just attempted to blow up. These changes
make the philosophical questions about human nature
more somber, if not bitter, for Todd is self-serving and
thoughtless, lacking in human compassion and emotion. The later edition is more faithful to an existential
and a nihilistic vision: The protagonist finds no good
reason either to live or to die—not religious belief, analytic reasoning, sexuality, humanitarian gestures, or
humor. The second edition also brings into clearer perspective the weaknesses, self-deceptions, and failings
of Todd himself.

Many early critics believe, as do Richard W. Noland
and Beverly Gross, that Barth's conclusion in *The Floating Opera* is a nihilistic one—that he finds little, if anything, of value.[2] Some find the nihilism as extreme as

Samuel Beckett's. Others play down that philosophical leaning and look instead, as does Charles B. Harris, to the presence of psychological probing or, as Harold Farwell does, to such moral values as love—"a creative attempt to be free from the prison of the self . . . as noble an affirmation as is the artist's comparable attempt to transcend his limitations in his art."[3] Yet a third interpretive position is represented by John Hawkes, Thomas LeClaire, and Campbell Tatham. As Tatham writes, "whatever else *The Floating Opera* may be about, it is fundamentally concerned with . . . the art of artistic creation."[4] As this critical debate suggests, the book *is* about nihilism, but it is also about love and art.

The main concerns of this first work are fundamentally related to the unsettling experiences of the twentieth century. Set in a thoroughly modernist context, *The Floating Opera* gives a sense of existential angst and world weariness, for as Heide Ziegler aptly notes, "Barth, like other fledgling contemporary writers, was influenced by the existentialist discussion which dominated the American intellectual stage of the 1950s."[5] Born in 1900, the main character, Todd Andrews, a lawyer from Cambridge, Maryland, is a product of the modern era: At the age of 18 he served in the First World War where, having fought and killed, he experienced its chaos and brutality; he was later stripped of the remnants of his personal security by the suicide of his father, who had lost the family fortune in the Crash of 1929. Since he has "no gods" and no stability other than Maryland beaten

biscuits—"few things are stable in this world. Your morn-
ing stomach, reader, ballasted with three Maryland beaten
biscuits, will be stable"[6]—Todd decides to commit suicide.

In the process of detailing the events and rationale
leading up to his aborted suicide, Todd provides an
overview of his attitudes that have, in a sense, remained
with him until the writing of the story in 1954. His experiences teach him that in general men and women are
not rational, but are animals driven by emotions, particularly mirth, sex, fear, and despair. His friendship
with Harrison Mack, Jr., and sexual relationship with
Jane Mack, Harrison's wife, instruct him in the nature
of the mind-body duality. This triangular relationship
is the first of many in Barth's books, which generally
illustrate the difficulties an individual has in pursuing a
steady course amidst life's complications.

One of Todd's primary goals is to find a guiding
philosophy or principle because he has lost his faith in
absolutes, due in large part to one traumatic experience
in World War I. During the war he was unable to function logically and found himself vomiting from fear:

Cowardice involves choice, but fear is independent of
choice. When the waves reached my hips and thighs I
opened my sphincters; when they crossed my stomach
and chest I retched and gasped; when they struck my
face my jaw hung slack, my saliva ran, my eyes wa-
tered. . . . But it was the purest and strongest emotion

I've ever experienced. I could actually, for a part of the time it lasted, regard myself objectively: a shocked, drooling animal in a mudhole. (63)

This fear brought him together with a German soldier who was alone in the trenches of the Argonne Forest. After their initial tussle, Todd gained the upper hand, sparing the German's life and then embracing him out of deep feelings of comradeship; they achieved what Nick Adams of Hemingway's *In Our Time* would have called a "separate peace." But after brooding over this situation, Todd came to fear this man and bayoneted him in an act of cold blood. This act caused him to realize his basic animality, to distrust himself and others, and to be skeptical of governing principles and systems of reason. Todd indicates that his loathsome action neutered him emotionally, symbolized by his final impotency with Jane Mack.[7]

In killing, Todd found himself and his system of values inadequate; he faced his generation's anxiety over a loss of belief in a protective God, a benevolent society, and a system of analytic reason. His awareness of death becomes his central concern and one of the principal metaphors of the book, but he is not as objective about death as he imagines. That he killed, that his father committed suicide, and that he has a heart condition mean that all his actions and thoughts are heightened by death. A few years after killing the soldier, Todd's discovery of his own heart condition makes him recognize his own vulnerability and mortality. This recognition seems in some obscure way to even the score, implicitly attracting him to suicide. He has so seriously absorbed the possibility of suicide that when Harrison Mack, apparently having lost his three-million-dollar lawsuit, speaks of not wanting to live, Todd sardonically quips: "What'll you do—hang yourself in the cellar? There's a twentypenny nail right there, in a joist—you'll find it. It's already been broken in" (99). This remark has an uncharacteristically bitter edge, revealing that Todd, too, shares anxiety on the matter of his father's suicide and his own inevitable death. He claims to have ruled out anxiety, but on the day of his planned suicide, he has three lapses of memory, makes a negative remark to Mr. Haecker about old age and death, and admits to horrendous despair the night before. He does not have the objectivity about death that he hoped to achieve.

Others, too, share Todd's preoccupation with death; these include Captain Osborn who is aware of his body's slow decay and death, as well as Haecker who, in holding too optimistic a view of the beauty of old age, is vulnerable to despair and eventually does commit suicide. Todd, then, lives each moment of life knowing that it could be his last:

This fact—that having begun this sentence, I may not live to write its end; that having poured my drink, I may not live to taste it, or that it may pass a live man's

tongue to burn a dead man's belly; that having slum-
bered, I may never wake, or having waked, may never
living sleep—this for thirty-five years has been the condition of my existence, the great fact of my life. (48)

The book deals with Todd's awareness, and anxiety,
concerning his possible death, so that when he decides
to commit suicide, it is with both fear and some relief
that something besides Maryland biscuits will at last be
stable and predictable.

While those such as Haecker feel futility regarding
death, Todd develops a sense of humor and cynicism.
He is unable to take seriously the human pretense to
rationality and belief in immortality. His feeling of the
absurdity of the human race is not only a product of his
participation in the war but also the result of other actions such as his unsuccessful attempt as a seventeen
year old to make love to Betty June Gunter. In trying to
seduce her, he suddenly saw himself in the mirror, "gan-
gly as a whippet and braying like an ass," and was
reduced to helpless laughter over the absurd image of
the "act of mating." From the time of this failed seduction and the war itself he could only think of men and
women as characterized by copulation and strife, not
by spirituality and logic.

It is Todd's sardonic humor in the face of death
that sets this book off from modernist treatments of the
inevitability of death. The humor here is not morose but
subtle, sardonic, witty, and sometimes wildly exuber-

ant. Todd makes himself, his disease, and death itself the objects of his humor: "To be sure, one doesn't want to live as though each day may be his last, when there is some chance that it may be only his next. One needs, even in my position, something to counterbalance the immediacy of a one-day-at-a-time existence, a life on the installment plan" (50–51). Confronting death may be inwardly sobering, but Todd carries it off with gamesmanlike panache. As Beverly Gross has commented, even despair in *The Floating Opera* is treated as a game.[8] The void left by an awareness of meaninglessness is partly filled by an awareness of absurdity. The seriousness of death is juxtaposed with copulating dogs, and romantic love is scuttled by its comparison to the "doubler" crab. Todd even laughs about the crab's taking longer at the sexual act than he does. Law, Todd's mind, the book itself, and human nature are compared to vaudeville in "ADAM'S ORIGINAL & UNPARALLELED FLOATING OPERA" (56).

Jacob Adam, the operator of this vaudeville show, is both a comical and divine figure, controlling the action on stage, portending disaster, occasionally frustrating the audience, later soothing and entertaining them, and inducing laughter. He serves as the master of ceremonies, conciliates the audience over the illness of Miss Clara Mulloy, fires the Shakespearian tragedian, T. Wallace Whittaker, and serves as the "Interlocutor" for the Ethiopian Minstrels. His show was to be the site of Todd's suicide, but served to interrupt it, negating his paralysis and providing Todd with energy after his paralysis and attempted suicide. In these various roles, Jacob undergoes several transformations "so that one doubted the authenticity of his original character" (257). Here, role-playing not only provides entertainment, but also ways to live and cope with absurdity. As his name biblically suggests, Adam is the first, a figure of mythic dimensions who manipulates and controls; he is the prime author in a comic drama. Through Jacob Adam's role Barth humorously deflates and demythologizes cultural beliefs and values, and delights in exposing the processes by which meaning is constructed—both the meaning of the patterns of life and literary style. The book goes beyond so-called black humor, which finds sardonic humor in the misfortunes of mankind, to confront death and animality and to discover delight in holding up cultural myths to laughter.

Part of Todd's realization of the absurd is his belief that great thoughts come from accident and chance, not from reason and planning. His flash of understanding regarding the Macks' trial comes when Miss Lake indecorously breaks wind while bending over in front of him. Todd links this fart to the 129 jars of feces collected by Harrison Mack, Sr., and constructs his plan to defeat Mrs. Mack. Similarly, his attempted suicide on board the *S.S. Thespian* is accidentally aborted, and Todd subsequently develops the rationale that he had no good reason to die. "My thinking," he says, "is always after the fact, the effect of my circumstances, never the other way round" (44). Reason for him is "du coeur" (of the heart), not of the head. When he tries to reason with his head, to provide an assessment of Betty June Gunter's enigmatic smile and murderous intentions, he finds plausible and conflicting reasons, without coming to a single conclusion.

Todd Andrews' claim to be a man of principle consequently arises from his awareness of the absurdity of life and a certain *joie de vivre*. Others' opinions of him as "eccentric and unpredictable" are true because his principles do not correspond with theirs and because his are based on the absurd and changeable, not the serious and stable. He finds *"no ultimate 'reason' for valuing anything"* (223). He makes a career of changing philosophies, and his way of thinking alters significantly in the fifty-four years of life leading to the writing of this first-person narrative. He confesses that each stage of his life has been marked by different principles or masks. After his innocence passes when he kills the soldier—and forever after hears the popping sound of the blade puncturing the skin—he becomes a devil-may-care, debauched university student. When brutally cut by Betty June, he changes dramatically from a "drunken animal" to a saint, in part again because he hears that small popping sound of mortality when the nurse punctures his arm with the needle. As a Buddhist saint of the "Esoteric variety" of "misanthropic hermitism," he believes he has to assume "hard control" over himself. That stance fails after his father's suicide, and he becomes a cosmic cynic. As a cynic, he is characterized by "no schedules, no demands, no jealousy, no fictions—all was spontaneity and candor" (161), but ironically it is during this period that he becomes impotent, suggesting that all is not well. The final mask, as Harris has remarked, is that of author, where he tries to explain his position to the readers.[9] These philosophical positions are the strategies he uses to interpret the central problems of his life. They are, he says, attitudes, stances, or masks that "represented the answer to my dilemma, the mastery of my fact; but always something would happen to demonstrate its inadequacy, or else the stance would simply lose its persuasiveness, imperceptibly, until suddenly it didn't work—quantitative change, as Marx has it, suddenly becoming qualitative change" (16).

His last position as a cynic demonstrates the problems of his various philosophical positions, because, while often affirming a governing principle, he finds many exceptions, though he sometimes denies them. As with his sailing, where he confesses that he can build a boat though he is unable to sail competently, he finds it easier to create a principle than live by it: "My daydreams, my conceptions of how things should be, were invariably grandiose, and I labored at them prodigiously and always secretly. But my talent for doing correctly the small things that constitute the glorious whole was defective—I never mastered first principles—and so the finished product, while perhaps impressive to the untutored, was always mediocre to the knowledged" (60).

THE FLOATING OPERA

Part of the problem of finishing his boats and adhering to water-tight principles lies in his intellectual curiosity and liberal spirit. He believes in choice and is sensitive to the variety of ways of interpreting reality and generating meaning, for "everything," he finds, "is significant." He is charmed by this idea and asserts that every new sentence is "full of figures and implications," though he has difficulty sorting out significances and reaching firm conclusions, because he "can understand everything at once in about three different ways." In the case of the word "love," for instance, he wonders whether it is possible to designate meaning: "Are the differences between, say, one's love for his wife, his mistress, his parents, his cats, his nation, his hobby, his species, his books, and his natural environment differences in kind, or merely in degree?" (36). He is ultimately unable to ascertain truth from words, because he learns that meaning is only attributable, nothing ultimately important, and the end irrelevant.

Todd sees no inconsistency in changing his principles, for he believes himself to have been relatively true to each one successively. He accepts each philosophical stance, each "mask," as real and vital with "life-or-death significance" until yet another idea, stance, or mask displaces it. Each, including Todd's meditated suicide, seems the best and final "solution," but each, in turn, is finally unpersuasive. He admits to changing or backtracking on many such assertions. His firm adherence to principles is, however, the rhetoric that he uses on the reader, one of the strong assertions that he usually has to recant or, at the least, qualify; his changing philosophical stances or masks are provisional. During the period of his sainthood, for instance, he admits to bedding the young "pieces" who thought him shy. He tells Harrison that he was a virgin and Jane that he loves her, but later confesses that he was simply telling them what he thought they wanted to hear. He thinks himself intelligent and calm, but the Macks find him hurtful. He says he had attempted suicide on June 23, 1937, and then admits to uncertainty about that date. He claims to have only one deformity—his fingers—and then describes his heart condition, infected prostate gland, and atrophied muscle in his left calf. His hyperbolic assertions are gradually withdrawn as he admits to the "little bits" and "almosts." During the World War I, he was bayoneted "just a little bit" by a German sergeant. He almost makes love to Jane Mack the first time before prematurely ejaculating. He is almost a sailor, though he never feels confident enough to take a boat out by himself. To declare himself healthy or bayoneted, a sailor or a lover, would be to accept and validate an absolute when everything tells him that there are no absolutes, that things are only more-or-less so. When he recounts his experience of retching animal-like out of fear in the midst of the battlefield, he comes to the conclusion that man is only more or less anything:

THE FLOATING OPERA

It is one thing to agree intellectually to the proposition that man is a species of animal; quite another to realize, thoroughly and for good, your personal animality, to the extent that you are actually never able to oppose the terms *man* and *animal*, even in casual speech; never able to regard your fellow creatures except as more or less intelligent, more or less healthy, more or less dangerous, more or less adequate *fauna*; never able to regard their accomplishments except as the tricks of more or less well-trained beasts. (63)

Because he can only view himself as an animal, not accountable for anything, Todd insists on his right to be irresponsible. He also comes to realize that his masks separated his heart from his mind, his emotions from his thoughts. He admits his rationalizing is a failure to integrate his bifurcated selves.

His view of law as a profession is based upon the view of man as more animal than rational. While interested in legal rules and the workings of courts, he considers law, and even justice, no more important than oyster-shucking. Being uncommitted, he is not concerned about guilt or innocence, right or wrong; he is only interested in an interesting case, a procedural dispute, or a labyrinthine affair.

Fundamentally related to Todd Andrews is his friend, Harrison Mack, who resembles him a great deal, though

Todd believes them opposites. Todd admits that in a rational universe, Harrison is the person he would most like to be. Harrison buys the house that Todd grew up in, shares his wife with Todd, and works with Todd on acquiring the Mack fortune. They also share similar views on principles—or lack of them. Todd accuses Harrison of having no real principles: he "adopts," says Todd, "the mood and manner of whomever he happens to be with. . . . He has no characteristic mood or manner of his own" (20). Todd thinks of him as a chameleon with the ability to adopt intellectual ideas and emotional colorings, but Todd confesses to Jane that he, himself, would say anything others want to hear. He also has to admit how fully committed Harrison has been to principles other than Todd's own. At the time that Todd was a saint, Harrison was an "out-and-out leaflet-writing revolutionary." When Todd became a cynic, Mack rejected Marxism and became a saint, speaking of the revolution in the soul and spirit of the individual, the " 'inner harmony' of the 'whole man.' " This sainthood is coupled with his objectivity, generous inclusion of Todd in his marital arrangements, and supposed lack of jealousy. When Harrison appears to be losing his trial, he suddenly discovers his materialistic, even capitalistic, side and is himself helped along by Todd from a belief in psychic determinism to cynicism.

What Todd reveals in comparing himself with Harrison is how little he probably understands his friend and how much he actually projects of himself onto Harrison. He claims that Harrison's emotions often varied from his ideas; that Harrison was emotionally troubled by the adulterous relationship he promoted between Jane and Todd; that, although saying Todd should not feel obligated over this sexual favor, he secretly wanted Todd to be obligated; and that, although Harrison claims no prejudices, he does not like blacks. The degree of accuracy in these statements is hard to assess because this is a first-person narrative, limited to Todd's own observations and impressions. His impressions are qualified by such adverbs as "doubtless" in order to make them more reassuring to the reader, but are shown to be biased. When Todd tells of the Macks' discussion about Jane's pregnancy, he describes it as a detailed recording of all that was said. He does occasionally insert "would" to indicate a hypothetical status, but by-and-large he tries to suggest that he was present. The degree to which Todd really comprehends Harrison is suspect. He sees Harrison as an extension of his own thoughts and wishes, a view that has led to the charge by several critics that Todd is a latent homosexual. More to the point, Harrison is Todd's sometimes approving and sometimes opposing double. If he fails to understand Harrison, he fails to know himself.

Also suspect are his reactions to Jane, whom he describes as beautiful, rich, athletic, sexually unparalleled, and comparable to a sleek sailboat. (Whatever he especially likes, whether his life, fiction, or mistress, he compares favorably to sailboats.) Caught between

Todd and Harrison, she is a lurking presence and pawn in their relationship. An emotional refuge for Todd, she does not seem to develop in the four years of their affair, but he still says little to individualize her. Initially, it is not clear whether that weakness is from Todd's preoccupation with his own life and proposed death, her own lack of depth, or Barth's failure to develop female characters adequately. Perhaps all are true. (Until his later fiction, *LETTERS*, *Sabbatical*, and *The Tidewater Tales*, Barth does not fully develop any female characters.) But in *The Floating Opera*, the main responsibility lies with Todd. In Todd's preoccupation with himself, he fails to see Jane as anything but a sexual object. Consequently, when Jane walks out on him, he is shocked, for he had not thought of her as a creature independent from his plans and lusts.

Despite Todd's predominant concern about comparing his, Harrison's, and Jane's lives, he is also interested in the nature of writing. He never disguises his function as a storyteller, and opens the book with comments that simultaneously refer to navigation and narration, of his intention to "stick to the channel" of writing and "let the creeks and coves go by." He also notes that fiction and life have mirroring qualities, though it is not clear which is the subject and which the reflection. He even introduces the chapter, "Calliope Music," with double, nearly mirroring, columns of type. He likes to share his knowledge of writing with the reader, admires the poetic turn of language that Froebel used in calling Harrison a "blue blood with a Red heart," and in the chapter "Coitus" smugly reveals that he is aware of climaxes and anti-climaxes both in sex and in fiction. He decries heavy-handed use of symbolism and foreshadowing by authors and prefers not to use them himself, because he does not find anything more than coincidentally symbolic. Although aware of and committed to writing, he is not as possessive of his writing as Harrison Mack, Sr., who could not bear to throw away his seventeen wills because they were his "soul-children"— like his jars of nail clippings and feces.

Todd's writing is of four genres—letters, legal discourse, biography, and autobiography. Todd tells the reader about his letters, legal discourse, and biography; the autobiography is *The Floating Opera* itself. The letters, which are only reported to the reader, are more imaginary than real, since they are never delivered. Before Todd's father committed suicide, Todd worked on a letter to explain his own heart condition. This *Letter to My Father*, which reached 50 pages, was never completed; his father died; and Todd was never able to overcome his imperfect communication. He tries to establish such communication with the reader through his self-inquiry, but that, too, is limited. In a real sense, after his "last correspondence" with the German soldier he killed, he cannot communicate with other people.

As a lawyer and writer of legal discourse, Todd is called upon to research and draw up cases for clients, but whether his arguments are ethical is not of fundamental importance to him; he takes cases out of interest, not justice, and his duty as a lawyer is to win those cases. He admits to the reader: No one "in Cambridge could bring suit against me with reasonable hopes of winning. In cases where I can't persuade judge or jury with rhetoric or legal gambit, I usually have something in my files to do the trick as evidence" (76). He is interested in the *bon mot*, not the *mot juste*, engages in "an admirable bit of casuistry" and rhetorical flourish, and professes that nobody cares about logic; people "make up their minds by their prejudices." He will play on a legal technicality to prove that Mrs. Mack, Sr., has violated the terms of the will by destroying 129 jars of feces. Arguing that law has nothing to do with justice, he will surrender the Morton-Butler case when the parties agree to settle out of court. The genre of legal brief consists, then, of giving speculative observations and questionable assumptions the ring of truth, to give legal fiction the shape of reality, and to give rhetoric the shape of legal reality.

The "life-inquiry and death-inquiry" is of a different order, for in it Todd tries to fathom the reasons for his father's suicide. He hopes that his father had other reasons than the loss of his fortune for committing suicide after the crash of the stock market in 1929. He reads numerous treatises, including Adam Smith's theories, to shed light on the economy and, by extension, his father's motives. He fills his room with notes in an attempt to arrive at solid reasons, the "key" to his father.

THE FLOATING OPERA

Reaching a decision is more difficult than he imagines, and requires "more lifetimes than it takes a lazy Buddhist to attain Nirvana." He is forced to admit that he cannot discover his father's real motivation and also that no one has the ability to be rationally objective. He comes to believe that "causation is never more than an inference," so his inquiry is basically pointless. In a sense, his role here is that of the judge rather than advocate, and he finds that he can make no ruling.

The most difficult genre for Todd is autobiography, because there he has to assess himself: his primary principles at any given moment, emotions that stand in the way of principles, and accidental circumstances that intervene to change his thoughts, actions, and principles. What he sets out to accomplish is simple: introduce himself, assess the book's title, and caution the reader against certain interpretations of his story; but he also attempts to defend his position. All of this he intends to do in leisurely fashion, to protect both his weak heart and the reader's.

The central occurrence of his autobiography, that which the rest of his study must consider and defend, is his attempted suicide in 1937. Although Todd is not an old hand at writing, he claims to know himself well enough that expression and interpretation pose no problems. Projecting an image that he is self-possessed about his life, if not wholly confident of an appropriate literary style, he announces that he can predict himself "correctly almost every time, because opinion here in Cambridge to the contrary, [his] behavior is actually quite consistent, and of course what is consistent is predictable." He adds that his actions "usually hang all in a piece, so that [his] life is never less logical simply for its being unorthodox" (1). But the reality of his writing shows that he has more difficulty assessing himself than he thinks. To be certain of himself, of his thoughts in relation to his actions, and to come to terms with his attempted suicide, he acquires seven peach baskets of material in nine years. This comprehensive investigation is ultimately shown to be futile; after editing his recollections and adding commentary and interpretations, he finally chooses portions at random every half hour to include in his autobiography. He also has to admit that he was not interested in truth or falsehood. What he betrays is the disjunction between his view of himself and others' views of him, between what he sets out to accomplish and what he finally produces, between planned, rational research and random selection and writing, between his heart and mind, and between fact and fancy. In that way he raises the question of whether he can ever be objective.

The question of objectivity in his autobiographical account is highlighted not only by the main issue of his attempted suicide, which many would consider irrational, but by the fact that he cannot remember precisely what day he attempted it. Such uncertainty raises questions about his entire manuscript, including the details he provides: although he claims to remember his exact clothing and each passing event of the day, how probable is that assertion? His failure to be convincing on this matter raises questions about many of his recollections and interpretations. He knows, for instance that *tod* is the German word for death, but feels that, since his name has two d's it might mean "almost death," offering a statement on his intended suicide. This interpretation, like that of all Barth's characters, easily attains the status of fiction, or misreading; rather than producing truth, all one can do is (mis)interpret.

The issue of Todd's ultimate lack of objectivity in his interpretations is conveyed by his style as well. Although he claims to be orderly and to stick to the channel, he does confess that he loses his path, that his narrative is a "meandering stream," that he digresses a great deal, and that there are probably gaps in his discourse: his is a floating opera "fraught with curiosities, melodrama, spectacle, instruction, and entertainment, but it floats willy-nilly on the tide of [his] vagrant prose" (7). The narrative is not self-contained and precise but sprawling, imprecise, and sometimes unfocused. Although sailing as a metaphor for writing runs through Barth's fiction from this first novel to the most recent *Sabbatical* and *The Tidewater Tales*, and indicates that fiction cannot be steered in a straight line, the tacking in *The Floating Opera* is to be seen as Todd's inconsistent behavior in the face of his belief in his own consistency. Sailing also signifies a tranquil retreat from the prob-

lems that beset him. When suffering from his undiag-
nosed prostate infection and being attacked by Betty
June with the broken bottle, he thinks, *"Why isn't the
whole thing a sailboat?* I remember wondering through
the pain that was crucifying me; then I could let go of
everything, tiller and sheets, and the boat would luff
up into the wind and hang in stays, and I could sleep"
(135). His behavior is inconsistent and cannot be mapped
like the Coast and Geodetic Survey of Dorchester County,
but is only like the walls of his room whose cracks resemble a map. Still, he is *trying* to tell somebody about
his life and views. As with Cicero, whom he quotes, a
large perspective on heaven and earth "wouldn't give
him much pleasure; but it would be the finest thing in
the world if he had somebody to describe it to" (167).
Todd's inconsistency in narration is, then, related to his
own inconsistencies, but he does enjoy telling stories.
Todd's assertion here reflects Barth's own that the art
of telling is much more important to the artist than what
is told. In an early interview he argues that an artist
must "come to terms with the discrepancy between art
and the Real Thing . . . to *affirm* the artificial element in
art (you can't get rid of it anyhow), and to make the
artifice part of your point."[10]

The way Todd shapes and distorts reality, trying
to map it out, can be seen in a related sense in his
discussion of his affair with Jane Mack. At first the Macks
show great pleasure including Todd in their sexual joys,

but Todd predicts that their attitude will change, where-
upon he notes that it does. He then draws up an out-
line, consisting of "Ante Coitum Felix" "The Act," "Post
Coitum Triste," and possible future directions. What
he has effectively done is to place this ménage à trois
within a traditional dramatic sequence; he has imposed
form upon his speculations, making life mirror a certain
conception of art.

An "opera" that carries Todd's reader on the meandering journey toward self-discovery, the "Inquiry" into
human understanding is never completed. What is included (or forgotten) is often inconsistent, discontinuous, and even inconsequential. The audience "could catch
whatever part of the plot happened to unfold as the
boat floated past, and then they'd have to wait until the
tide ran back again to catch another snatch of it. . . . To
fill in the gaps they'd have to use their imaginations"
(7). According to E. P. Walkiewicz, *"The Floating Opera*
is a work of fiction that denies our attempts to view it
as a focused and accurate reflection of reality that drifts
free of things as they are."[11] Because communication is
imperfect, normal, rational, continuous attempts at communication are impossible. Todd never tells his father
about his heart problem; Todd's father never explains
his suicide; Jane never tells Todd the reasons for the
Macks' decision to withdraw Jane's sexual favors; Todd
never tells Morton his reasons for suddenly giving him
$5,000. The book denies one's ability to live by rational

principles, to assess life rationally, and even to communicate fully those limitations. As Ziegler remarks, this piece of communication is sent to the reader as a substitution for the one Todd never sent to his father—or for the one his father never sent to him. In this role as author, Todd becomes the informing father and the reader the surrogate son.[12] Todd has, in the process, opened up a channel, muddy as it may be.

The Floating Opera is not, then, exactly nihilistic nor wholly about love or art. It explores the fragmentary nature of art and life and the inconsistency of human action. When Todd tries to look at others such as his father or best friend, Harrison, he sees the shadow of himself. He casts that same reflection over his relationship with Jane. These people are not real to him, except as he describes them and prescribes their activities (much like Barth the author to his characters). Whether Todd judges his father's death, himself, or his writing, he finds questions dominating answers, death overshadowing life, and incoherence sabotaging communication. This realization sometimes renders him inert, but the writing of *The Floating Opera* allows him some measure of responsibility, freedom, and even insight.

THE FLOATING OPERA

Notes

1. Enoch P. Jordan, *"The Floating Opera* Restored," *Critique* 18 (Winter 1976): 6–7.

2. Richard W. Noland, "John Barth and the Novel of Comic Nihilism," *Contemporary Literature,* 7 (Autumn 1966): 239–57. Beverly Gross, "The Anti-Novels of John Barth," *Chicago Review* 20 (1968): 3.

3. Charles B. Harris, *Passionate Virtuosity: The Fiction of John Barth* (Urbana: University of Illinois Press, 1983) 11–31. Harold Farwell, "John Barth's Tenuous Affirmation: 'The Absurd, Unending Possibility of Love,'" *Georgia Review* 28 (1974): 290–306.

4. John Hawkes, *"The Floating Opera* and *Second Skin," Mosaic* 8 (1974): 17–28. Thomas LeClair, "John Barth's *The Floating Opera:* Death and the Craft of Fiction," *Texas Studies in Literature and Language* 14 (Winter 1973): 711–30. Campbell Tatham, "John Barth and the Aesthetics of Artifice," *Contemporary Literature* 12 (Winter 1971): 60–73.

5. Heide Ziegler, *John Barth* (London: Methuen, 1987) 13.

6. John Barth, *The Floating Opera* (rev. ed., Garden City, N.Y.: Doubleday, 1967) 53. Further references will be noted parenthetically in the text.

7. Stanley Edgar Hyman, "John Barth's First Novel," *The New Leader* (12 April 1965): 20–21, interprets this neutering to mean that Todd is the victim of an Oedipus complex.

8. Gross 3.

9. Harris 18.

10. "John Barth: An Interview," *Wisconsin Studies in Contemporary Literature* (Winter–Spring 1965): 6.

11. E. P. Walkiewicz, *John Barth* (Boston: Twayne, 1986) 26.

12. Ziegler 22.

CHAPTER THREE

The End of the Road

Like *The Floating Opera, The End of the Road* was revised and republished in 1967, a year of reworkings for the author. Unlike the first book, the second did not require major structural shifts—only a little fine tuning. This wish to make changes indicates a significant trend for Barth—to recast old material into new forms. Barth calls this technique orchestration and improvisation, "arranging" established discourses in his own way for his own purposes.[1] Over the years, the author has recycled his own earlier material, and he has taken images, stories, and symbols from many works, including *The Odyssey, The Thousand and One Nights,* and Greco-Roman myths, locating them firmly within his native Maryland. The revisions are perfectly in keeping with Barth's continuing interest in nihilism, relationship between art and reality, and the correspondence between sex and the author/reader. Of these nihilism is predominant in *The End of the Road.*

Whereas the major events of *The Floating Opera* take place in 1937, just at the end of the Great Depression and before the onslaught of World War II, *The End of the Road* takes place in 1951, just after the war as the United States had to find new economic, political, and moral directions. Reminders of the angst and milieu of war in both books are evident in many ways. Both protagonists are nihilistic. Todd Andrews of *The Floating Opera* is invigorated by it, but Jake Horner, the narrator of *The End of the Road*, is enervated by that same nihilism. Todd searches for answers to questions and causes for effects, but Jake assumes no single answer or cause exists; everything is equally plausible and, therefore, beyond choosing. Whereas Todd dons his philosophical masks to escape the paralysis resulting from his killing of the German soldier and the suicide of his father, similar masks keep Jake from making solid decisions or recognizing the finality of death and absurdity of life. In this way, Jake's inertia and masks become the tragic mirror image of Todd's.

The main characters of *The Floating Opera* and *The End of the Road*, indeed the books themselves, become doubles, for Barth thinks of these two as a pair: one a nihilistic comedy and the other a nihilistic tragedy.[2] The basic nihilistic principles of Todd Andrews are contrasted in *The Floating Opera* with those of Harrison and Jane Mack, while in *The End of the Road* the nihilistic Jake Horner is set against the rationalist, existential Joe Morgan and his emotional wife, Rennie. Because of this dualistic opposition, which implies psychological as well as philosophical divisions, Charles B. Harris argues that the book "reflects Barth's interest in schismatic selfhood"; David Kerner thinks of the book as a psychodrama; and Daniel Majdiak, using Barth's own affirmation of parody from "The Literature of Exhaustion," holds that Jake is the parodic double of Joe.[3] Heide Ziegler, too, considers this book a parody—of the existential novel, and a replenishment of the form that *The Floating Opera* exhausts. She does not think of Barth as "the moral teacher of humanity,"[4] but there is a seriousness in the book that her view of parody ignores: the nihilism here is more intense than in *The Floating Opera*. The tongue-in-cheek quality of Barth's later parodic fictions is absent, and *The End of the Road* remains Barth's darkest book. Although much of the angst is initially covered by Jake's manic moods and verbal responses which are inappropriate to the weight of the problems he creates, that humor cannot disguise the despair at the end of the book.

A young university graduate, Jacob Horner has had problems establishing goals and directions. He has found so many choices available that he finds no particular one compelling. His name itself exemplifies this ambiguity. In an interview, Barth remarks that Jake Horner's name is simultaneously drawn from the nursery rhyme (Jack Horner) and cuckolding conventions (to give or to be given "horns").[5] Such ambiguity of names and lack of motivation and direction imply that Jake has no identity or purpose. As a consequence, his doctor advises him to take a position teaching prescriptive grammar, which he assumes is uncomplicated and will prove a stabilizing influence because of its emphasis upon rules and logic. Following that advice, Jake becomes involved in a friendship with another teacher, Joe Morgan, and sexually involved with his friend's wife, Rennie. Jake's inability to make decisions and to keep from lying and playing games results in Rennie's tragic death on an operating table in the midst of an abortion. The fact of death brings Jake's games to a sudden close; it strips bare his various masks and reduces him once again to immobility, which only the writing itself may ease.

Jacob Horner has a history of paralysis. Unable to finish his M.A., he sat on the bench of the Pennsylvania Railroad Station in Baltimore, ran out of beliefs and motives, and ceased moving. Like his statue of the Laocoön, his eyes "were sightless, gazing on eternity, fixed on ultimacy," what he calls "the malady *cosmopsis.*"[6] He sees no values in life, and he thinks of himself as a frog blinded by the hunter's light, but fails to realize that as he imposes his nihilism upon others, he becomes the hunter, as destructive of himself as others. He may be able to visualize "the lead slug waiting deep in the chamber" for Rennie Morgan, but that does not make him perceive his own responsibility.

Not believing in an authentic self, Jake loves to play various roles. At the same time, he wants to play God, for as he says: "[W]e are all casting directors a great deal of the time, if not always, and he is wise who realizes that his role-assigning is at best an arbitrary distortion of the actors' personalities" (25–26). He preserves for himself the role of the enlightened one, assigns lesser roles to others, and labels their "essences." At certain points he recognizes the distortion this causes—"Assigning names to things is like assigning roles to people: it is necessarily a distortion, but it is a necessary distortion if one would get on with the plot, and to the connoisseur it's good clean fun" (135)—but then continues to assign roles anyway. When he cannot immediately assign a role to a person, as with Rennie, he sets out clinically to observe reactions. "My mood," he says, "was superior, in that I regarded myself as the examiner and her as the subject" (47). He even informs the reader of his familiarity with such psychological techniques as "the non-directive" approach in order to show his grounding in psychology and his right to scrutinize people. In this way, he looks at them as objects and himself as subject. His practice is hardly benign. He toys with and manipulates people, thinking of them as animals in a lab, as indicated by his referring to Rennie as an "unharnessed animal," even saying, "Whoa, now!" when she breaks into tears (52, 53). His view of Rennie as an animal is only slightly more refined than his description of another teacher, Peggy Rankin, as a "Forty-Year-Old Pickup," whom he treats like a prostitute.

Jake's therapist warns him about labeling people, and Jake himself believes that as he gets to know people his attitudes soften. Even so, when he seduces Rennie for the second time (at Joe's command), he resorts to labeling Joe, Rennie, and himself:

Joe was The Reason, or Being (I was using Rennie's cosmos); I was The Unreason, or Not-Being; and the two of us were fighting without quarter for possession of Rennie, like God and Satan for the soul of Man. This pretty ontological Manichaenism would certainly stand no close examination, but it had the . . . virtue of excusing me from having to assign to Rennie any essence more specific than The Human Personality, further of allowing me to fornicate with Mephistophelean relish. (123)

Such labeling ultimately brings Jake to the brink of disaster and puts him back in the hospital following the death of Rennie and his own subsequent commital to the Remobilization Farm. "Remobilization" is an appropriate term to designate the therapy administered to Jake, for he has been utterly paralyzed by his responsibility for Rennie's death. Before that, he has floated through situations without commitment or responsibility. When Rennie is beside herself, questioning the basis of their sexual relationship and feeling that she has destroyed a fine marriage with Joe, Jake thinks it is "funny as the devil." He is even flattered when Rennie admits she loves him, and he brushes aside her comment that she also hates him. He is insensitive and disrespectful of others.

His opening comment, "In a sense, I am Jake Horner," implies a tentativeness of life and attitude. At one time he confesses that his most recurrent problem is to discover that on certain days he has no "weather" or emotional moods or intellectual drives: "On these days Jacob Horner, except in a meaningless metabolistic sense, ceased to exist, for [he] was without a personality" (33). He had no ego. Emotionally, he claims to be melancholic—a "placid-depressive: a woofer without a tweeter"—and only rarely does he manage zest and humor. One of these occasions is the first day of school at Wicomico when he participates in the "dance of sex," the celebration of "the Absolute Genital"; but this occasion is short-lived for Joe destroys his mood by confronting him with charges of adultery. Another occurs when Rennie comes to make love and is altogether cheerful. Her cheer dispirits Jake, but when he manages to dampen her joy, he becomes happy, a vampire sucking the emotional and intellectual spirits from others.

What he does not always realize is the extent to which he changes emotional and intellectual positions. On many occasions his "successive and discontinuous selves" do not hang together, and as he acknowledges, his "attitude toward Joe, Rennie, and all the rest of the universe changed as frequently as Laocoön's smile: some days I was a stock left-wing Democrat, other days I professed horror at the very concept of reform in anything; some days I was ascetic, some days Rabelaisian; some days super-rational, some days anti-rational" (61).

He also observes that he can, with "perfectly equal un-
enthusiasm," simultaneously hold conflicting responses.
He does not view these as paradoxically reconciled, for
a paradox to him is "a really arresting contradiction of
concepts whose actual compatibility becomes percepti-
ble only upon subtle reflection. The apparent ambivalence of Rennie's feelings about me, I'm afraid, like the
simultaneous contradictory opinions that I often amused
myself by maintaining, was only a pseudo-ambivalence
whose source was in the language, not in the concepts
symbolized by the language" (135). Within the context
of Barth's works, this ambivalence to conflicting attitudes is a trait typical of all human beings, who are
basically inconsistent, despite their attempts at consistent self-identity. But Jake's inconsistency is more acute,
for, as he says: "It seemed to me that the Doctor was
insane, and that he was profound; that Joe was brilliant
and also absurd; that Rennie was strong and weak; and
that Jacob Horner—owl, peacock, chameleon, donkey,
and popinjay, fugitive from a medieval bestiary—was
at the same time giant and dwarf, plenum and vacuum,
and admirable and contemptible" (114). He does not
want to reduce these contradictions, nor to erase the
differences that should be maintained, but this double
perspective is crippling for him, and these mercurial
variations are taken to such an extreme that he, more
than any character, has no identity. Rennie is, in many
ways, the most perceptive regarding him and comments
that he hardly exists: "You know what I've come to

think, Jake? I think you don't exist at all. There's too many of you. It's more than just masks that you put on and take off—we all have masks. But you're different all the way through, every time. You cancel yourself out. You're more like somebody in a dream. You're not strong and you're not weak. You're nothing" (62–63). His therapist notices much the same thing and, when Jake appears especially confident, implies that Jake is at best a shadow or reflection of someone else. He is, perhaps, even a reverse solipsist: instead of the world reflecting him, he reflects the world. His relationship with Peggy Rankin bears out this observation, for in it Jake tries to emulate what Joe did to Rennie: he tries to convince her that he wants an uncommon relationship based on respect; he even socks her in the jaw as Joe did to Rennie as an indication of his desire for honesty. Peggy, however, sees him as altogether solipsistic: "You're so wrapped up in yourself that you don't have a shred of respect for anyone else on earth!" (89). She finds that Jake puts her in false, humiliating positions.

Accompanying Jake's self-centeredness is his belief that nothing is absolute and everything relative, although it "doesn't follow," he says, "that because a thing is unjustifiable, it's without value" (35). He questions convention after convention—being invited to dinner by the Morgans on two successive days, having to make small talk with Peggy before seducing her—and ultimately, in committing adultery with Rennie, breaks the sacrosanct vows of marriage. But the breaking of conventions has the same devastating effect on him as murder and fear had on Todd. Jake exclaims, "the guilt poured in with a violent shock that slacked my jaw, dizzied me at the wheel, brought sweat to my forehead and palms, and slightly sickened me" (96). Despite his intention to set aside common morality, he feels embarrassment and shame, and has to think of himself as an adulterer, deceiver, betrayer of friends, and coward. This guilt leads to contemplated suicide.

Jack claims to have no values, but discovers the effects of conscience; he wants to be a cynic, but cannot accept the responsibility. When he tries to arrange the abortion for Rennie with Dr. Welleck, he invents elaborate lies to get the job done and himself off the hook. His undergraduate background highlights this avoidance of responsibility and direction. With no major, he has weakly pursued a liberal arts and science program, taking various subjects without fulfilling any particular requirements or establishing any goals. When he comes to find a profession, his therapist insists that he have more objectivity and stability, a "body of laws" to guide him, the kind of stability that plane geometry or prescriptive grammar would provide. But, as Jake well knows, mathematics is not limited to plane geometry nor is grammar to the prescriptive; relativity, arbitrary conventions, "optional situations," and historical accidents have their places in the pantheon of ideas. That awareness proves detrimental, for Jake cannot always function well without order and some body of laws. He may be able to argue with his student, Blakesley, about the necessity for enforcing conventions and the freedom from convention paradoxically provided by following the rules, but he cannot live that way. He can neither dispassionately break conventions nor abide by them; he can neither laugh at conventions while living them nor discard them. As a modern man, he is caught between the need for laws and the knowledge that there is no absolute order, but his doctor lays the responsibility fully at his door: "If you'd studied your *World Almanac* every day," he says, "and thought of nothing but your grammar students, and practiced Sinistrality, Antecedence, and Alphabetical Priority—particularly if you thought them absurd but practiced them anyway—nothing that happened would have been a problem for you" (171).

Although Jake seems candid to the point where he will admit to having no strong emotions or governing philosophy, his style of narration suggests subterfuge. It is true that he is sometimes candid about artifice in his narrative,[7] but more often his comments cloud rather than clarify. Whereas Todd of *The Floating Opera* playfully informs the reader of his quest for an appropriate narrative style, Jake views "telling" as a "kind of therapy." Nevertheless, he rarely talks about his style; he prefers to keep the discussion centered on abstractions, observations of others, and his varying moods, but he rarely confesses that his rhetoric conceals rather than discloses his motivation. For example, when questioning Rennie about Joe's hitting her, he admits to feeling some degree of sympathy and then qualifies it: "This sympathy, too, I observed impersonally and with some amusement from another part of myself, the same part that observed me being not displeased by Rennie's tearful, distracted face" (52). His response is schizophrenically divided, but he passes himself off as objective and coherent before labeling Rennie's account of her life as commonplace. His mask of objectivity slips, and he reveals the stereotypes that dominate his mind and continue to influence his action. Although his doctor reminds him that "not only are we the heroes of our own life stories—we're the ones who conceive the story" (83), he does not wholly share that view. He overstates positions and falsifies them, and then valorizes those positions: "To turn experience into speech—that is, to classify, to categorize, to conceptualize, to grammarize, to syntactify it—is always a betrayal of experience, a falsification of it; but only so betrayed can it be dealt with at all, and only in so dealing with it did I ever feel a man, alive and kicking" (112–13). His is probably a position that Barth himself endorses, but coming as it does from Jake, who falsifies so much, it registers ironically.

Horner can be seen as Jacob wrestling with God, trying to wrest authority and project meaning in a world devoid of values. In this respect, he shares many of the main features of Todd in *The Floating Opera* and is part of the same mythic structure, for as Jake tells the readers, "The same life lends itself to any number of stories—

parallel, concentric, mutually habitant, or what you will"
(4). Similarly, Jake's conception of himself as a quester
for meaning is juxtaposed against the roles of Joe and
Rennie Morgan in much the same way as Todd is played
off against Harrison and Jane Mack. This ménage à trois
allows for comparing certain intellectual positions and
attitudes. In an interview Barth is quite explicit about
this usage: "One of the images that . . . recur through
my novels, is . . . the pair of opposites—the two men in
the triangles are usually contraries."[8]

Joe's and Jake's names hint at a close identification
or doubling, which Rennie articulates: "You're *not* totally different from Joe: you're just like him. I've even
heard the same sentences from each of you at different
times. You work from a lot of the same premises" (59).
But while the two men are intellectually similar, their
attitudes toward themselves and others are for the most
part opposite, a doubling that David Kerner thinks is
"Self against Non-Self, Identity against Protoplasm, the
Real against Vacuum. The contest of body and soul,
shadow and substance, chaos and order, devil and God
suggest a medieval allegory: and Barth provides the bat-
tleground that God and devil need—the cosmos to affirm and deny. . . ."[9] Jake believes in nothing and has
no goals, and consequently, he has difficulty in making
decisions. Joe does not believe in anything transcenden-
tal or ultimate but affirms the primacy of reason. He
heads directly for his destination and claims that he will
not even hesitate to kill himself, Rennie, or Jake if some-

thing interferes with his ideals. (Ironically, it is Jake's general inconsistency that kills Rennie.) He has steadfast beliefs and generally practices communally-held virtues. He "had a look about him that suggested early rising, a nutritious diet, and other sorts of virtue" (17). His conventional virtues go hand-in-hand with his philosophy that, although nothing may ultimately matter, things do matter "immediately." Joe rejects cultural absolutes, but embraces those values that work for him personally in his specific context. "Less-than-absolutes" are necessary and good because they allow the self and others of a given society to function with sufficient ease. He settles for the pragmatics of a well-run household and society.

Joe does not, however, believe that all conventions are governed by "unity, harmony, externality, and universality." "In my ethics," he says, "the most a man can ever do is be right from his point of view; there's no general reason why he should even bother to defend it, much less expect anybody else to accept it, but the only thing he can do is operate by it, because there's nothing else. He's got to expect conflict with people or institutions who are also right from *their* points of view, but whose points of view are different from his" (42). This he calls "American pragmatism" and "cheerful nihilism" as opposed to the more dour and less practical French existentialism. These go together with his view of American innocence and energy—the topic of his Ph.D. dissertation. They also agree with his views on free choice.

Joe's virtues are engendered by his native brilliance, and he tries to keep his "normal ebullience" under firm, rational control. Intellectually versatile, he argues politics, history, music, ethics, and logic. But he cannot altogether maintain that discipline; although at times he appears noble, strong, and brave, at other times he is, as Jake maintains, "completely ridiculous. Contemptible. A buffoon, a sophist, and a boor. Arrogant, small, intolerant, a little bit cruel, and even stupid. He uses logic and this childish honesty as a club and a shield at the same time. Or you could say he's just insane, a monomaniac: he's fixed in the delusion that intelligence will solve all problems" (117). He is also perverse in forcing Rennie to visit Jake and make love to him against her will. He is even more perverse in the aftermath of Rennie's death when he tries the same tactics of analysis that he tried concerning her seduction. These aberrations are demonstrated in one of the pivotal points of the novel when Rennie and Jake observe him cavorting about his room, simultaneously picking his nose and masturbating. The intellectually and socially unified veneer cracks, exposing the animal behavior that lies just below the surface. He seems not to understand how much human beings are motivated by their animality.

Like Jane Mack of *The Floating Opera*, Rennie is caught between the two protagonists and seems to have little identity of her own, but she is given a depth that was denied Jane. Whereas Jane was sophisticated, svelte, and beautiful, Rennie has a strong kind of clumsy, animal beauty. Jake maintains that "it was a clumsiness both of action and of articulation—Rennie lurched and blurted—and I was curious to know whether what lay behind it was ineptitude or graceless strength" (47). He admits, however, that though "she could not handle her body in situations where there were no rules" (50), she is superb at football. With a build and resourcefulness that are often associated with maleness, she would appear to be a match for both Jake and Joe. Certainly, she intimidates Jake when he first meets her. With forcefulness, candor, and wit, she confronts him on his refusal to come to dinner. She seems to have the "beast *honesty*," and Jake laments to himself that she has aborted his "infant manic." This "beast" continues to dominate her, and she will not settle for Jake's lies in arranging for her abortion.

It is true that Rennie is often insistent and thoughtful, frequently making Jake feel uncomfortable with her probing questions, but, in part, that is because Jake always wants to turn situations into intellectual sparring matches, putting abstract considerations on non-logical conventions, occurrences, and feelings. She so intimidates him that he imagines himself the prey and she the predator, while in reality the situation is reversed: It is he who preys on her sexually, destroys her marriage, and is ultimately responsible for her death.

Rennie's physique and apparent resourcefulness belie her basic insecurity and vulnerability. She is, in fact, dominated by both Joe and Jake. She yielded to Joe almost from the start: because he told her she was empty-headed, she dismissed her friends, drew away from her parents, and effaced herself completely so that she could embrace his way of life, which she considered superior to her own. Jake admits that this emptying of herself fascinates him: "I think Rennie's attraction for me lay in the fact that, alone of all the women I knew, if not all the people, she had peered deeply into herself and had found *nothing*" (62). In Jake's estimation, she has not constructed a new self but has become a pale reflection of Joe: "Rennie Morgan, though lively, seemed to be just a trifle unsure of herself; her mannerisms—like the habit of showing excruciating hilarity by squinting her eyes shut and whipping her head from side to side, or her intensely excited gestures when speaking—were borrowed directly from Joe, as were both the matter and the manner of her thinking" (29). Rennie's habit of whipping her head is, however, profoundly hers and suggests the extent to which she is affected by pain or laughter. She whips her head to show feeling, not to arrive at an intellectual position. Her fundamental humanity will not be denied, but her pact to stay with Joe as long as they can be intellectually honest and open puts great pressure on her to analyze all events in the same logical way that he does, for she has to follow exactly his pattern of thought. (Although Joe often views her as self-sufficient, strong, and private, he does not realize the extent to which he reads these qualities into her: she is the text and he the reader, bringing meaning.) Joe even

assumes that he has the right to bully Rennie into coming to his conclusions: "If I straighten Rennie out now
and then, or tell her that some statement of hers is
stupid as hell, or even slug her one, it's because I respect her, and to me that means not making a lot of
kinds of allowances for her" (42). Joe considers himself
the doctor who will cure Rennie's diseased mind.

After a few days of seeing how much Rennie respects Joe and builds her life around his conceptions,
Jake begins to probe her attitudes, and she opens up to
him. In his own coldly logical way, he, like Joe, views
her as a patient and himself as her psychologist. Such
an attitude is clinical and revolting, and what Jake fails
to comprehend is that Rennie was never "empty," a
tabula rasa, but had been systematically erased by Joe
and himself. Just as Joe previously tried to dissuade
Rennie from her youthful, carefree ways, so Jake tries
to convince her to ignore Joe's lead. He manages to
undermine her resourcefulness, put into doubt her own
integrity, and demonstrate that Joe is more animal than
rational. In the book's pivotal scene, where Rennie and
Jake peek at Joe masturbating, Rennie has her illusions
about Joe's sustaining rationality and perfectibility
stripped from her. Her carefully constructed trust in
him collapses, and she is reduced to nothingness, left
"wordless, grammarless," alienated and lonely. To be
wordless is not necessarily bad, for Rennie says in a
moment of insight that "I think all our trouble comes
from thinking too much and talking too much" (125);

but having lived so long in someone else's mental structures, she lacks options. Her great sensitivity and warmth of affection are voided by this revelation. She argues the merits of Joe's and Jake's positions, but never once does she seem to realize that she could, like Jane of *The Floating Opera,* simply step out of others' logical systems; that she could choose options that neither man gives her does not occur to her.

After both Joe's and Jake's viewing Rennie as a patient, it is not surprising that she dies at the hands of another doctor. Jake's mythotherapist has no business operating on her, because he has not been medically trained. He may be effective in helping Jake to understand the "knowledge of the world," choice, and action. He may even be right in arguing that "human existence precedes human essence," but he has no right to interfere with the life of Rennie, no more than Joe and Jake have had the right to interfere with her emotions and mind. One system of thought or human endeavor cannot double in other situations, for that brings destruction and death.

The integrity of one system must exist by itself. Jake, Joe, and Rennie are independent agents; nihilism and existentialism are no substitute for genuine human emotion; art and life are separate endeavors. Each has its possibilities and limitations and ought not be confused or blended in one's mind. Rennie's emotions do not have to be converted into Joe's rational structures. And Joe's rational structures do not have to succumb

THE END OF THE ROAD

to Jake's nihilism. Art can teach us about life, a view that Barth has repeatedly confirmed, but it is not life. Differences need to be sought and protected, and the transcendent reconciliation of opposites and hint of "mystical unity"[10] do not materialize. This is something that neither Joe, Jake, nor the mythotherapist understands. Had they understood it, people like Rennie would not become their victims, nor would Joe ultimately have become Jake's victim.

Notes

1. John Barth, "Some Reasons Why I Tell the Stories I Tell the Way I Tell Them Rather Than Some Other Sort of Stories Some Other Way," and "My Two Muses," *The Friday Book: Essays and Other Nonfiction* (New York: Putnam, 1984) 7, 159.

2. Barth, "Some Reasons," *The Friday Book* 3; and David Morrell, *John Barth: An Introduction* (University Park: Pennsylvania State University Press, 1976) 13.

3. Charles B. Harris, *Passionate Virtuosity: The Fiction of John Barth* (Urbana: University of Illinois Press, 1983) 32. David Kerner, "Psychodrama in Eden," *Chicago Review* 13 (Winter/Spring 1959): 59–67. Daniel Majdiak, "Barth and the Representation of Life," *Criticism* 12 (Winter 1970): 51–67.

4. Heide Ziegler, *John Barth* (London: Methuen, 1987) 17–18, 30.

5. "John Barth: An Interview," *Wisconsin Studies in Contemporary Literature* 5 (Winter–Spring 1965): 12.

6. Barth, *The End of the Road* (Garden City, N.Y.: Doubleday, 1967) 69. Further references will be noted parenthetically in the text.

7. Harris 40.

8. Alan Prince, "An Interview with John Barth," *Prism* (Spring, 1968): 56–57.

9. Kerner 64.

10. Harris 48.

CHAPTER FOUR

The Sot-Weed Factor

*T*he *Sot-Weed Factor* (1960) and *Giles Goat-Boy* (1966) mark an abrupt shift from the predominantly realistic strategies of *The Floating Opera* and *The End of the Road*. The extended, mostly linear treatment of despair and nihilism gives way to a more extravagant engagement both with ideas and forms of fiction. These are the big novels of Barth's middle two decades of writing and constitute his most sustained, protracted effort to write and unwrite the novel. Each has a specific literary form that it palinodically uses—the historical romance and the epic: the long, expansive novel is both produced (written) and parodied (unwritten).[1] Each has a related philosophical purpose. In its exuberant rewriting of the John Smith-Pocahontas story, *The Sot-Weed Factor*—the title refers to a tobacco merchant—questions the traditional notions of American history. *Giles Goat-Boy* engages classical philosophy and Christian theology, showing that they consist more of narrative than essential truth.

In order to address these large concerns Barth needs

large books, but their size is not an attraction to all readers. Many find the volumes too massive for enjoyable reading, and they contend that the subplots often overwhelm the plots. The threat that the subplots about Burlingame or early Maryland politics will overwhelm the main plot of Ebenezer's development in *The Sot-Weed Factor* is a real one, for Barth devotes as much energy and space to contextual details as he does to the primary plot. Barth states two reasons for the heft of *The Sot-Weed Factor:* "One was to write a large book, something that the publisher could print the title on across the spine. . . . The other was to see if I couldn't make up a plot that was fancier than *Tom Jones.*"[2] Because Barth wanted to outdo *Tom Jones,* he needed to write a protracted work full of plots, subplots, stories, and stories within stories, not to mention sermon-like discourses on an abundance of topics. To accomplish this task, he incorporated general stories about America's founding as well as the specific development of politics in Maryland.

The Sot-Weed Factor mixes invention, history, and myth as well as self-conscious speculation about ways to produce and understand those different kinds of writing. Stock literary characters and minor historical figures are woven together in scenes that are sometimes fantastical and sometimes realistic. Ebenezer Cooke, for instance, was someone who actually did exist, but about whom little is known. As David Morrell points out,[3] there were few accounts of Cooke, a late seventeenth-

THE SOT-WEED FACTOR

and early eighteenth-century man; only one essay, Lawrence Wroth's "*The Maryland Muse* by Ebenezer Cooke"[4] offered a biography of him. A barrier to a historian, the scarcity of details about Cooke did not deter Barth, whose chronicling of events in *The Sot-Weed Factor* owes more to eighteenth-century fiction, not to mention twentieth-century fiction, than it does to eighteenth-century fact. The genuine roots of the colonizing of America, though, are not ignored; they serve as a strong foundation for the fictive construction of Cooke. Several critics of *The Sot-Weed Factor* suggest that the theme of historical origin is an important one. Charles Harris, for example, believes that Barth chose the seventeenth and eighteenth centuries because they marked significant changes in social and scientific attitudes, and Alan Holder respectfully treats the issue of Barth's extensive rewriting of history.[5]

Barth's vivid embellishment of America's colonization is what remains memorable in this long novel. Cooke's journeys between England and America are, among other details, his invention. No doubt a reader hastening through *The Sot-Weed Factor* to absorb the plot will be overwhelmed by the fictional account of Ebenezer, who was supposedly born in America while his father was an agent for an English manufacturer. The estate called Malden that Cooke's father built in Maryland becomes a special object of Ebenezer's desire, the embodiment of all the material possibilities offered by the New World. The special relationship between Cooke and his sister, Anna, who are educated in England and then embarks on a quest to America, is also a major concern within the novel. Their love for each other, bordering on incest, and their desire to possess Malden are treated with the same tone of comic seriousness as is Cooke's hope to be the poet who will celebrate America. As for the historical backdrop of the novel, Barth fictionalizes both Lord Baltimore and John Coode, who were major figures and combatants in Maryland politics, mixing interpretations of their actions to such a degree that Cooke cannot finally decide the merits of either.

Playing loosely with historical documents does not, however, mean that Barth could produce the novel effortlessly. Morrell reports that with only half a first draft completed in early 1958, Barth had amassed one thousand manuscript pages. Morrell also reveals that *The Sot-Weed Factor*, because of its length, initially encountered editorial skepticism, then, on publication, sold poorly, and was subjected to scathing reviews. Terry Southern wrote in *The Nation* that sections of the book "seem designed, specifically, to *bore one to tears*."[6]

Although Cooke, the book's major figure and author of an actual poem called "The Sot-Weed Factor," is a legitimate historical figure, Henry Burlingame III, of uncertain parentage, is an invented shape-shifter who assumes many names and at least eight guises in the course of the novel. At the beginning of the novel he is Ebenezer's tutor. Part of his name emphasizes "game," and the other part, "burl," emphasizes the weaving and unraveling of narrative: burl is an uncommon word meaning to finish cloth especially by repairing loose threads and knots. Certainly, whenever the plots reach intractable or knotty stages, Burlingame appears in one of his personae to unravel what had gotten Ebenezer into his fix. Such is the plot's format, with enough knotting and unraveling to ensure that Burlingame is always the major force in explaining what has transpired.

Barth himself burls history freely and richly, taking various events and stories about the founding of America and giving them a fictive gloss, restoring the fabric that is history's necessary complement. In a coda of sorts, the author provides a theoretical commentary on the relationship of history and fiction:

Lest it be objected by a certain stodgy variety of squint-minded antiquarians that he has in this lengthy history played more fast and loose with Clio, the chronicler's muse, than ever Captain John Smith dared, the Author here posits in advance, by way of surety, three bluechip replies arranged in order of decreasing relevancy. In the first place be it remembered, as Burlingame himself observed, that we all invent our pasts, more or less, as we go along, at the dictates of Whim and Interest. . . . Moreover this Clio was already a scarred and crafty trollop when the Author found her. . . . But if, despite all, he is convicted at the Public Bar of having forced what slender virtue the strumpet may make claim

to, then the Author joins with pleasure the most engaging company imaginable, his fellow fornicators, whose
ranks include the noblest in poetry, prose and politics. . . .[7]

Clio, the muse of history, is depicted as no innocent,
no neutral assessor. "Pure" history is impossible.
Ebenezer's own purity, his own virginity, which is comically and extravagently held until the novel's closing
scenes, is finally surrendered to the syphilitic Joan Toast.
Neither Ebenezer nor history can survive unscathed in
a fallen world.

Accordingly, stories that are legitimized as history,
as well as the theories of histories themselves, are reevalu-
ated in *The Sot-Weed Factor*. One of the chapter titles late
in *The Sot-Weed Factor* is "The Poet Wonders Whether
the Course of Human History Is a Progress, a Drama, a
Retrogression, a Cycle, an Undulation, a Vortex, a Right-
or Left-Handed Spiral, a Mere Continuum, or What Have
You" (679). Reading the world continuously, seamlessly
or, indeed, in any interpretable manner at all via history
is what Barth attempts to subvert here. He shows that
history and mythology are both subordinate to and com-
prised of narrative and are dependent, in part, on techniques of fiction for impact and even validity. The Author,
as Barth calls himself, mixes the *History of the Voiage Up
the Bay of Chesapeake* with the false *Privie Journal of Sir
Henry Burlingame* to adulterate history and fiction. Tales
of missionaries and the legend of Pocahontas are irrev-
erently and uproariously altered. The story of Pocahon-

tas, for instance, gets rewritten and augmented to include how a tribe called the Ahatchwhoops choose their king. Involved is an eating contest in which ritualistic contests and the epic relating of them are themselves parodied. Barth's delight in storytelling here far outstrips the narrative needs of the novel; in fact, it is the digressions from characters' tales that give the novel its bulk. In order to save themselves, Captain Smith's crew depend on Burlingame, the largest member of that crew, to win the eating contest as proxy for one of the "salvages" against Attonce, another rival for kingship and the hand of the Pocahontas figure, Pokatawertussan.

At sight of her, Attonce let goe a mighty hollowing and Burlingame . . . he was so taken with her, that he shook all over, and slaver'd over his lippes and sundry chinnes. . . . Attonce then commenced to slap his bellie with his hands, to the end he might arouse a grander of lust for food, and seeing him, Burlingame did likewise, until the rumbling of their gutts did eckoe about the swamps like the thunder of vulcanoes. (562)

Thereupon foods are presented—an epic list that allows ample space for Barth's comic invention. Attonce and Burlingame eat monumentally and evenly until Attonce, having "let flie a tooling fart . . . dy'd upon the instant" (564). Smith then jumped up and popped one last berry into Burlingame's mouth, making him the victor. Carousing and caressing mark the victory celebration and the end of the journal's entry. This scene is a wonderful one for the energy of its author, the scope of his parodies, and the use of epical forms. Political tales of the settling of Maryland and the securing of and conniving for power, social tales of marriage, and sexual doings of the late seventeenth and early eighteenth century— these Barth recounts and augments in *The Sot-Weed Factor* with wit and gusto.

The single most important insight to be drawn from the attempts to build history through coincidences and recurrences is that to explain those parallels is to burl a game, to invent a fiction. Thus, Barth's long novel, which is really a series of stories related to and centering on Ebenezer, is itself its justification, a rejection of solid identities, definitive plots, answers.

Barth's treatment of history is only one of the two main concerns of the novel. The other is the notion of the development of the hero. Heide Ziegler deals with the question of Ebenezer's and Burlingame's identity, asserting that the book is Barth's ironic parody of the motif of the protagonist's maturing,[8] and John O. Stark thinks the book refutes the belief in essential, unified identity.[9] Much of *The Sot-Weed Factor* is concerned with the quest for identity: Ebenezer's as a poet, Burlingame's as a son. The structure of the novel is that of a three-part initiation story. The first part begins with Ebenezer's idealistic fancies about life, love, and poetry and with his education in England. His self-pronounced identity as poet and virgin is constantly challenged, however, especially in the second part of the book, as Eben makes his way to Malden. All his assumptions and beliefs are questioned, and he, like Todd Andrews in *The Floating Opera*, has to face up to the reality of animal instincts. The recognition brings despair about life and cynicism about poetic ideals, and it is not until the last section of the novel, in which he spends time with the Indians, that he is able to accept his own and the rest of humanity's failings. Only then can he write his poem, earn his plantation, and marry.

In this treatment Barth does not produce a novel that shores up identity. For him identity is not something solid, obtainable, and desirable; the values surrounding it are inflated and constructed. Thus, the postmodern inversion of solid values and revered traditions is pursued. Ebenezer complains to Burlingame that some unknown is going around claiming to be him, Maryland's Poet Laureate: "he hath robbed me of myself; he hath poached upon my very being" (188). Burlingame responds, "Thourt talking schoolish rot. What is this coin, thy *self*, and how hath he professed it?" (188). Burlingame, ever Ebenezer's tutor, reiterates this motif some time later when, traveling in one of *his* many guises, he is told by Ebenezer that he looks more like himself than he did on an earlier occasion. Asserting that the world is "a happy climate for imposture" (330), Burlingame goes on to say that Ebenezer's notion of a "true and constant Burlingame lives only in your fancy, as doth the pointed order of the world. In fact you see a

Heraclitean flux: whether 'tis we who shift and alter and dissolve, or you whose lens changes color, field and focus: or both together. The upshot is the same . . ." (330).

Ebenezer's twinship with Anna helps to undermine the notion of individually achieved identity. The two are only halves, and their lives, in fact, are incomplete until they are reunited near the end of the novel and likened to husband and wife as they live together, raising the child of Burlingame and Anna as their own. Early in "Part III: Malden Earned" Henry lets the ever-zealous Ebenezer know that he, Ebenezer, has been mistaken in regarding Henry as being the object of Anna's desire. Deflecting accusations of trysts with her, Henry says that Ebenezer is her true love.

Ebenezer's astonishment and horror at such incestuous notions are the occasion for Henry's speech on twins called "A Cosmophilist." This chapter heading alone should be warning enough to anyone trying to place the twinning motif at the center of *The Sot-Weed Factor* specifically or all Barth's works generally. Burlingame's learned disquisition, which spills over into a celebration of numerous twins named in three densely packed pages (some of whom are actual and others of whom are invented), provides an ironic commentary on the meaning of twins in history, civilization, and literature. Ebenezer, as Burlingame discovers at great length, can only interject such comments as "A surfeit! . . . There is a surfeit!" (495). This pandect, or complete treatise on the subject, pronounced by a cosmophilist, or someone with a magnified view of the world—remember Nabokov's injunction that "cosmic" is always in danger of losing its "s"—is a *tour de force*. Henry begins with the notion that twins long always for the closeness and bliss of prenatal completeness: "As Aristophanes maintained that male and female are displaced moieties of an ancient whole, and wooing but their vain attempt at union, so Anna, I long since concluded, repines willy-nilly for the dark identity that twins share in the womb, and for the well-nigh fetal closeness of their childhood" (489). Celebrating the metaphorical dimensions of twinning, Henry goes on to list the twins' sacred letters: A,C,H,I,M,O,P,S,W,X, and Z. The letter H, for instance, "portrays the same happy union of two into one: 'tis the zodiac sign for Gemini; the bridge 'twixt the twin pillars of light and dark, love and learning, or what have you: 'tis also the eighth letter, and inasmuch as 8 is the mystic mark of redemption (by virtue of its copulating circles), 'tis no surprise that H is the emblem of *atonement*—the making of two into one" (493). Surely, here, Barth the game player is having fun with his readers, teaching them to distrust portentous interpretations. All of the designs of criticism can be seen to be as farfetched as this reading of 8 and H. All such seemingly learned explanations of signs and events are being mocked by Barth.

Burlingame's role in the novel is parallel to Ebenezer's. Indeed, he serves to mock Ebenezer's conceptions of a self-unified personality. Burlingame is not only tutor to Ebenezer in the clouded, interpretatively complex ways of the world, but he also enacts comically and self-consciously the quest for lineage, parentage and, therefore, legitimacy. The emphasis on Burlingame's name highlights the linkage between propriety and legitimacy. Much postmodern fiction and theory perversely elevate the illegitimate and the improper. Burlingame, too, follows the well-worn path of literary heroes such as Tom Jones, who search for legitimate identity and proper parentage. But Barth's by-now-familiar parodic way undercuts the importance of such a discovery of truth. Burlingame begins life as an orphan, like Moses in the bullrushes, discovered in an otherwise empty canoe, with only his name, Henry Burlingame III, written on his skin.

Unraveling that plot and trying to discover his identity, his origins, propels Burlingame back and forth across the Atlantic until, in America, he discovers his link with the Ahatchwhoops. In addition to substantiating his paternity, he finds the recipe for a dried eggplant aphrodisiac that provides him the potency he previously lacked due to a minuscule penis. Restored to family and sexuality, he fathers a child by Anna, Ebenezer's twin sister, then disappears, late in the novel, back to the Ahatchwhoops. Such farfetched doings destabilize the importance of authenticating one's identity. Northrop Frye writes that the loss and regaining of identity is literature's preoccupation, and certainly one of the mod-

THE SOT-WEED FACTOR

els for *The Sot-Weed Factor* is based upon that view: The eponymous hero of *Tom Jones* is, as the full title indicates, a foundling through much of the novel, seeking his rightful place in a society that will only accept him fully if he can find his lineage, his roots, and prove them to be befitting a gentleman. But for Barth it is only one model among many—and one to unwrite as well as to write. The latter occurs because, despite the fact that Burlingame's quest is detailed hyperbolically and farcically, it does proceed with a kind of correctness. After all, Burlingame bemoans his orphan status all the while deriding proper names. In addition, it is only upon discovering his lineage that he weds and reproduces, giving his line the kind of continuity that Tom Jones himself sought. Moreover, Burlingame's departure makes his role in the novel much more purely literary; he is, as are all characters in Barth's fiction, the novelist's convenience, to be dispatched as the author sees fit—and the reunion of Ebenezer and Anna, the twins, is what Barth wishes to leave his readers with at the end of *The Sot-Weed Factor*.

This consideration of Ebenezer's and Burlingame's identities relates to Barth's treatment of character generally. His characters are consistently de-created; that is, attempts by readers to conceive of them as realistic, rounded characters are frustrated by the author. In "The Medium of Fiction," Gass writes, "That novels should be made of words, and merely words, is shocking really. It's as though you had discovered that your wife were made of rubber: the bliss of all those years, the fears . . . from sponge."[10] Despite the wealth of details about the Maryland of the eighteenth century, and despite allusions to Ebenezer's growth or Burlingame's quest for his personal history, Barth is by no means writing traditional historical fiction in which a historical landscape is invented so that realistic characters can frolic authentically in it. Rather, these characters, who change implausibly from one identity into another and reunite due to one coincidence after another, manifest their creator's wit. He has not produced progeny that are fully formed, autonomous creatures, but rather has produced words on a page to highlight and parody various ideas and conventions. For Burlingame truly to find his father he would have to confront Barth himself!

Barth is, at once, a reader and parodic producer of early American documents as well as eighteenth-century novels. In this latter guise, he emulates Henry Fielding. In an interview about *The Sot-Weed Factor* Barth stated:

One of the interesting things about eighteenth-century fiction, about the early novel, is the author with a capital "A," that fellow who intrudes. . . . Fielding's novels pretend to be this, that, or the other thing—anything except that it should be a piece of *fiction*. . . . I thought it might be interesting to write a novel which simply imitates the form of the novel, rather than imitating all these other kinds of documents. In other words, it pretends to be a piece of fiction.[11]

THE SOT-WEED FACTOR

What Barth is referring to near the end of his remarks is the tendency of novelists such as Fielding to label their works histories—as in *The History of Tom Jones, Foundling*—and load them with verisimilitude or the texture of daily life, in short, to write novels as if they were reports that use language realistically. Insecure about its form, so Barth obviously felt, early practitioners of the novel had to claim affinities with a supposedly more serious and authentic genre, history, but their characters were patently drawn from literature. So are Barth's Joan Toast, the prostitute with "a heart of gold"; Bertrand Burton, the unscrupulous, calculating valet; and Ebenezer, himself, as innocent physically as Tom Jones is culturally. These are figures who gain their force from their literary predecessors, not from Barth's eye for contemporary profiles and personalities. In another novel that uses, as *The Sot-Weed Factor* does, crudely drawn characters, and that depicts women as whores or virgins, Indians as savages, and blacks as sexual athletes, the stereotyping would be unconscionable. Barth's purpose, however, far from being to exploit these figures, is to reveal their stylized, artificial qualities, the dubiousness of anchoring any identity or stereotype in reality.

To rewrite the eighteenth-century novel Barth had to provide an ironic rewriting of *Tom Jones*. Ebenezer Cooke's innocence, the temptations he encounters in the form of alluring women, an education and career fraught with wrong turns and faulty judgments—these are elements found in both novels, but treated more respectfully in *Tom Jones*. The quester in *The Sot-Weed Factor* finds on that relatively "new" continent all of the political and social intrigue and the vices Tom Jones had to deal with in England. Gaining and losing friends, gaining and losing Malden, his father's estate, Cooke recapitulates Tom Jones's journey from innocence to experience. Tom Jones's initiation is, by and large, the major purpose of Fielding, but the plot of *The Sot-Weed Factor* is overwhelmed by multiple stories, so that the book is denied a unified plot even as Ebenezer is denied a unified personality. Fixed meanings and incremental discoveries give way to the fictive merry-go-round on which Cooke is placed. Explanations he gets are always patently artificial and extravagant.

The way Barth gives this novel the meandering pace of an eighteenth-century novel—itself a desire to recover an indulgent pace that is irrelevant to a realistic novel— is to present few actions except as they are related by the characters in the novel. Stories, narratives, tales are the most frequently recurrent activities in *The Sot-Weed Factor*. The journals of Smith and Burlingame I are mixed with stories told by all sorts of characters to a usually incredulous Ebenezer. Ever the innocent, narratively as well as experientially, he at one point urges Henry to complete a story more hastily than Henry was doing: "Prithee put me off no farther on the matter; I must know whether the odyssey bore fruit!" (146). Burlingame responds: "Make not such haste to reach the end,

THE SOT-WEED FACTOR

Eben; it spoils the pace and mixes the figures. Whoever saw an odyssey bear fruit?" (146). Unless one reads slowly, caressingly, forgivingly, as story within story unwinds unhastily, the odyssey in *The Sot-Weed Factor* will bear the reader no fruit. Like Ebenezer, the reader must learn to receive the stories raptly and avidly, allowing the pace and direction to be determined by the teller.

Barth's stories portend no understanding of history, no development of human psychology, no morals regarding the propriety of Ebenezer's virginity or Burlingame's chicanery, no plot resolution that justifies the approximately eight hundred pages of storytelling. Yet here is a novel that need not, as Barth avers *Tom Jones* does, require the justification as anything *except* fiction. While the poem, "The Sot-Weed Factor," that is Ebenezer's life's work and that is offered in bits and pieces throughout the novel, contains rhymed couplets verging on doggerel, it is only an excuse for the less purposeful but more pleasurable forays of *The Sot-Weed Factor*. Early in the novel Ebenezer is granted the title "Poet and Laureate of Maryland," and feels pressed to live up to his title as laureates are required to do by producing occasional verses, that is, poems demanded by authorities to commemorate some extraordinary event or place. Happily, Barth is as free of any such obligations as he is of Fielding's constraints. In *The Sot-Weed Factor* he subverts Clio, the muse of history, and substitutes no utilitarian goal or god in her place.

Notes

1. Heide Ziegler (in *John Barth* [London: Methuen, 1987] 31, 64), comments extensively on Barth's parodies of fictional forms.

2. John J. Enck, "John Barth: An Interview," *Wisconsin Studies in Contemporary Literature* 6 (1965): 6.

3. David Morrell, *John Barth: An Introduction* (University Park: Pennsylvania State University Press, 1976) 34.

4. *Proceedings of the American Antiquarian Society* 44 (October 1934).

5. Charles B. Harris, *Passionate Virtuosity: The Fiction of John Barth* (Urbana: University of Illinois Press, 1983) 54; and Alan Holder, "What Marvelous Plot . . . Was Afoot? History in Barth's *The Sot-Weed Factor*," *American Quarterly* 20 (1968): 596–604.

6. "New Trends and Old Hats," *The Nation* 191 (Nov. 19, 1960): 381.

7. Barth, *The Sot-Weed Factor* (New York: Doubleday, 1967) 679. Further references will be noted parenthetically in the text.

8. Ziegler 31–39.

9. John O. Stark, *The Literature of Exhaustion: Borges, Nabokov, and Barth* (Durham, N.C.: Duke University Press, 1974) 118–75.

10. William Gass, *Fiction and the Figures of Life* (New York: Knopf, 1970) 27.

11. John Barth and Joe David Bellamy, "Having It Both Ways: A Conversation Between John Barth and Joe David Bellamy," *New American Review* 15 (April 1972): 149–50.

CHAPTER FIVE

Giles Goat-Boy or, the Re-vised New Syllabus

In *Giles Goat-Boy* Barth continues to deflate my-thologies, not just of the self and the origins of America as in *The Sot-Weed Factor*, but of periods that are para-doxically both more contemporary and yet more histori-cally removed. He has chosen a modern university setting, but his locus is the Bible, through which he parodies what seems to be the entire spectrum of West-ern (and some Eastern) thought. When the novel was in progress, Barth wrote, "What I really wanted to do after *The Sot-Weed Factor* was a new Old Testament, a comic Old Testament. I guess that's what this new novel, *Giles Goat-Boy*, is going to be about. A souped-up bi-ble."[1] His souped-up Bible is a playfield for the inver-sion of theological, mythological, philosophical, politi-cal, and literary concepts.

Giles Goat-Boy is as long and complex a novel as *The Sot-Weed Factor*. The main body of the novel, though it taxes a reader's patience, does not tax his or her capac-ity to understand what is happening. *R.N.S. The Revised New Syllabus of George Giles, Our Grand Tutor*, reads, despite its digressions and density of allusions, as the personal disclosures and inspirational messages of a prophet. As in *The Sot-Weed Factor*, myth and history provide the nucleus that Barth augments and embellishes. Speculation about the legitimacy of myth, history, and fiction again plays an important role in the novel. Barth mentions in an interview with David Morrell in *John Barth: An Introduction* that *Giles Goat-Boy* took him five years and three months to complete, approximately twice as long as it took him to write *The Sot-Weed Factor*. The reason for this, he said, was that "while the matter of *The Sot-Weed Factor* was more complicated, the manner of *Giles* was more difficult. But once the narrator's voice was worked out, the writing came swiftly."[2] Barth had to solve the dilemma of giving Giles both ancient and modern dimensions as well as both prophetic and carnal qualities. Barth's achievement is to make Giles seem both divine and human, profound and humorous.

Another of the author's successes in *Giles Goat-Boy* is his entertaining and unpedantic presentation of scholarly material. As he states in a lecture read on December 10, 1964, at the State University of New York at Genesco and published in *The Friday Book* as "Mystery and Tragedy: The Twin Motions of Ritual Heroism," Barth happened to read Lord Raglan's famous treatise called *The Hero* after he was finished writing *The Sot-Weed Factor*. He was fascinated by Raglan's discovery of "the *pattern* of mythic heroism as it seems to occur in virtually every culture on the planet."[3] Raglan presents a detailed list of prerequisites, twenty-two in all, to qualify as a mythic hero.

Another model for heroic status that Barth discovered soon after reading Raglan's book was *The Hero with a Thousand Faces* by Joseph Campbell. With their theoretical formulations of heroic patterns in mind, Barth adapts them in a comic, updated way to Giles, his protagonist in *Giles Goat-Boy*.

When it was published in 1966, *Giles Goat-Boy* became an alternate selection of the Literary Guild and even appeared on some best-seller lists. Perhaps because of its university setting or its irreverent rewriting of all that rebellious university students of the time were supposed to keep sacred, the book was especially popular on campuses. Along with *Steppenwolf*, by Herman Hesse, and *Slaughterhouse-Five* and *Cat's Cradle*, by Kurt Vonnegut, *Giles Goat-Boy* became a cult novel. For students of literature weaned on the serious treatment of symbols, mythical patterns, and allegory, the book contained the right mixture of profundity and cheekiness. World War I and II, the Cold War, sin and redemption, Moses and Christ, body and soul, tragedy and comedy, religion and atheism are thinly disguised in *Giles Goat-Boy* so that young readers could, and can, grapple with them in casual, "hip," unpedantic ways.

To list all of the characters in *Giles Goat-Boy* would be to replicate the roll call for much of the world's influential literature and mythology. Nonetheless, the book's thread or continuity is fairly simple. The material that

UNDERSTANDING JOHN BARTH

precedes and follows the R.N.S. of "George Giles, Our Grand Tutor" is meant to call into question the authenticity of that purportedly Biblical work. It also provides an ironic commentary on how such a spiritually important work would be received by a skeptical twentieth-century audience. The *R.N.S.* catalogs Giles's doings. His ambiguous birth, innocence and naivety, tutoring by Max Spielman, struggles with the boyish and goatish dimensions of his character, and the sexual, social, and philosophical aspects of that mixed heritage are the focuses of the early "reels"of the *R.N.S.* Because this Bible is contemporary, the book is said to be tape-recorded rather than put directly into print. Bluntly asserting that he would be a hero and a "Grand Tutor," Giles sets off on the quest that will gain him knowledge and martyrdom, that will help him discover Good and Evil or, in academic terms, Passédness and Flunkédness. Almost immediately, he gets into trouble. Saving Anastasia, who will be his companion throughout the rest of the "reels," he encounters Stoker, the novel's devil figure, who stokes the furnace in the hellish bowels of the physical plant. Other major events are his witnessing of *The Tragedy of Taliped Decanus*, Barth's rewriting of *Oedipus Rex*; his friendship with Peter Greene, the novel's "down-home" American; a decadent party orchestrated by Dr. Sear; confrontations with the antiChrist Bray; various tests, including his descent into WESCAC's belly (a giant computer that is the dynamo of the Western Campus), to determine his worthiness of canonization.

GILES GOAT-BOY

This book is a satire, not only on the desire to become a hero, but of the literary conventions that serve to shore up the presentation of heroic deeds. Some critics, such as Robert Scholes and Charles B. Harris, are less concerned about the nature of satire and more interested in the way that Barth explores oppositional structures and endorses the principle of synthesis, both with regard to theme and structure—the book's form is essentially thesis, antithesis, and synthesis.[4] Several characters are dialectically paired: Eierkopf, the "egghead," tries to measure and quantify life, whereas his opposite, Croaker, embodies instinctive drives; Stoker, who runs the physical system of the university is dark and interested in raw physical power, while Rexford, the administrator, is light and seeks the power inherent in academic structures; George is youthful, positive, and innocent, and Bray is older, negative, and experienced; Peter Greene is from the West and his counterpart, Leonid Andreich Alexandrov, is from the East, each sharing the blindnesses of his society. Jac Tharpe places synthesis or parodoxical resolution at the forefront of the motifs and unifying themes. The oppositions of America and Russia, West and East, light and dark, Eierkopf and Max are paradoxically resolved.[5] But the balances of those resolutions are not equally achieved in all instances: Max and Eierkopf cannot really be integrated, nor can East and West.

As James Gresham has observed, in exploring heroism, Barth chooses both a religious hero and a tragic hero—Jesus Christ and Oedipus Rex.[6] George Giles, fluctuating between the *salvator mundi* (savior of the world) instinct and the desire for self-discovery, operates simultaneously on both levels. As savior, George is a god, around whom Barth has arrayed fragments from various religions to create this archetypal figure. His father is WESCAC, the novel's god-figure, and his mother is Virginia Hector, a virgin. His confrontation with Bray is a confrontation with the devil. He is related to spring, dawn, order, fertility, vigor, youth, whereas Bray is associated with winter, darkness, sterility, confusion, moribund life, old age.[7] In the climactic tower scene Bray is described as having a black cape and being older-looking than in earlier scenes in the novel. His semen is a glaucous thick substance. The cohabitation of Bray and Anastasia parodies the epiphanic moment, the time of sexual union, which takes place in the tower. The tower, in turn, is associated with the omphalos—"the earth's navel, the point at which creation began."[8]

Bray, though, is necessary to George—"it was his *function* to be driven out."[9] George reiterates this when he says, "I have to drive him out of the Belly now . . . and sooner or later off the campus. Part of my work" (668). The confusion in the identities of George and Bray reflects the difficulty of knowing and separating the divine from the demonic: A number of times George wears a mask of Bray, and at one point Bray dons a goatlike mask. The bourgeois society is easily duped as to the identity of the real savior. Bray as a mythic being has supernatural powers. Also, because he is already damned, he can enter WESCAC's belly without trepidation. His ostentatious, miraculous properties make him more appealing as a divine hero than George who, like Christ, is the Word made Flesh—who takes on the characteristics of a human and is tortured by the hostile crowds. Yet it is George who, when he dies, will receive what Northrop Frye calls the solemn sympathy of nature which is accorded a dying god: "My parts will be hung with mistletoe, my cleft hold the shophar fast; the oak will yield, the rock know my embrace. Three times will lightning flash at a quarter after seven, all the University respeaking my love's thunder—*Teruah! Tekiah! Shebarim!*—and it will be finished. The claps will turn me off. Passed, but not forgotten, I shall rest" (708). Even here, however, Barth has mitigated adoration of Giles by placing this prophecy in the possibly specious "Posttape." Indeed, the whole question of the efficacy and legitimacy of George the Messiah is left hanging. The world may not be ready for a savior, even if he is genuine. George knows the reaction that awaits his prophecies, his Grand Tutoring. A few will attend him. "The rest will snore in the aisles as always, make paper airplanes from my notes, break wind in reply to my questions" (707). Despite adolescent errors and also the scoffing of critics and the well-intended misrepresentation of disciples, he believes in his Messianic, Grand Tutorial self. Although he appears mad to studentdom, he ventures into the belly of

WESCAC. Without being able to know whether his act is significant, he undertakes it.

One further facet of George's action on the anagogic level is particularly significant: his relationship with Anastasia. Their preliminary encounters are more lustful than religious. In fact, in the climactic scene of "Reel Two" the sacred sexual act they later perform in WESCAC's belly is parodied. George and Anastasia are placed on the dais in front of the revelers at Stoker's orgy, during the "Sunrise Service." Aided by the libidinous Sear, they are readied for their ritualistic consummation.

> "In the name of the Founder," I declared, *"and of the sun-"*
> *"Ole!"* they cried behind me.
> *"—and of the Grand Tutor so be it!"*
> Incredibly as I mounted home, the music swelled and rose to bursting. As ever in goatdom, the service was instant: swiftly as the sunflash smiting now the Founder's Shaft I drove and was done. Anastasia squealed into the cushion, "I *do* believe!" and fell flat. (199)

The religious quality of this passage is unmistakable; in the context of their later lovemaking it is also ironic. Moreover, this moment is not sexually fulfilling for Anastasia; she does not get pleasure from intercourse. Also, she does not conceive a child.

Anastasia's impregnation in WESCAC's belly provides the culmination of *The Revised New Syllabus*—in sexual and religious terms simultaneously. First, there is Anastasia's transformation, the submission of her will to a superior. George tests her:

"Assert yourself, Anastasia," I ordered huskily, to test her. In a very positive small voice she answered: "No."
I stepped to her, stirred to the marrow, and kissed her lips. Like Truth's last veils our wrappers rose: her eyes opened; I closed mine, and saw the Answer.
"Pass you!" I whispered. She nodded. (672)

One cannot mistake George's Grand Tutorial nature in this passage; Anastasia in turn, can be seen as a divine instrument. "I the passer, she the passage, we passed together, and together cried. 'Oh wonderful!' Yes and No. In the darkness, blinding light! The end of the University! Commencement Day!" (673). George has completed his personal quest. His search for Commencement Gate, enunciated in the first paragraph of *The Revised New Syllabus,* has ended triumphantly. Second, there is the nature of George's and Anastasia's consummation. In WESCAC's belly, the two lovers are united ("I and My Ladyship, all, were one" [673]) as an androgynous figure. "'It says ARE YOU MALE OR FEMALE,' she whispered. We rose up joined, found the box, and joyously pushed the buttons, both together, holding them fast as we held each other" (672). Together they remind

UNDERSTANDING JOHN BARTH

one of a hermaphroditic deity: "[The concept of hermaphrodite] expresses in sexual—and hence very obvious—terms the essential idea that all pairs of opposites are integrated in Oneness. . . ."[10]

Wrestling with religious issues, with belief in a deity, with spiritual concerns is, of course, a universal preoccupation. Nonetheless, especially in novels popular with students in the late 1960s and early 1970s, the search for different options in terms of religion was prominent. In Vonnegut's *Cat's Cradle*, for instance, Bokononism, a comical, inverted kind of Christianity is held up as an alternative to orthodox religions. In *Giles Goat-Boy* one of the world's great religions is treated as fiction, as artifice, allowing for the renewed questioning of values and seeking of answers. *Giles Goat-Boy* satirically adulterates theology, mysticism, and spirituality with fiction. Barth does not dismiss the divine out of hand. *Giles Goat-Boy* does not have an atheistic focus; indeed, atheism is presented as being as much of a style or construct as any religion. Instead, the novel insists on the narrative and cultural dimensions of divinity.

George Giles is not only a religious figure, but also a tragic hero. Despite Harold Bray's appearance at the end of *The Tragedy of Taliped Decanus* in which he shouts "Taliped Decanus and his sort are flunked forever! Tragedy's out; mystery's in!" (314), the Oedipus legend permeates the novel. *Giles Goat-Boy*, in fact, fluctuates between the poles of mystery and tragedy. In the "Post-

GILES GOAT-BOY

script to the Posttape," J. B., somewhat like Harold Bray, bewails the shift from mystery to tragedy that the George of the "Posttape" undergoes: "Having brought us to the heart of Mystery, 'He' suddenly shifts to what can most kindly be called a tragic view of this life and of campus history" (710). In the "Posttape" George foresees that his ending, orchestrated by nature's solemn sympathy, will also have affinities with Taliped's expulsion from Cadmus. George will be taken from New Tammany College, "naked, blind, dishonored" (707).

The difference between the religious figure and the tragic hero is that the latter is human. Frye states that such a hero is subject both to social criticism and to the order of nature. Thus, the story of George as a tragic hero is one that features ordinary rather than superhuman occurrences. Also, his story has universal significance; it is one with which humans can empathize. It provides insight into the lives of men and women and into their relationships with nature. Dr. Sear interprets Taliped's actions for George at the end of *Taliped Decanus:*

Committed and condemned to knowledge! That's the only Graduation offered on West Campus, George—
We all flunked with the first two students in the Botanical Garden, George; we're committed to Knowledge of the Campus, and if there's any hope for us at all, it's in perfecting that knowledge. (313)

Read as a tragedy, the *R.N.S.* records a movement from innocence to experience, from concealment to insight. George, like Oedipus, willfully innocent and passionately honest, persists in learning his parentage. He also remains committed to his loftiest goal, changing WESCAC's aim. Although on this level WESCAC's aim is fixed, unmovable, George's heroic attempts to remedy an irremediable human situation lead to a greater understanding of that situation. He is that genuine tragic hero who sacrifices himself and all that is his for the universal. *Giles Goat-Boy*, then, has it both ways: it presents a hero who is not bound by mortals' concerns, and it presents a hero who confronts and must submit to ethical considerations.

Other avenues of play need not be overlooked in *Giles Goat-Boy*. Interested in authorial presence and intervention or invention, Barth teases readers about the relationship of himself to J. B. and of J. B. to the scheme of the novel. J. B. is jaded with his own life—"Yesterday one was twenty; tomorrow one dies of old age" (xxix)—and with his art—"To move folks about, to give them locales and dispositions, past histories and crossed paths—it bored me, I hadn't taste or gumption for it. Especially was I surfeited with *movement*, the without-which-not of story" (xx). He rejects the cause-and-effect world of realists. J. B. yearns to be George, the author of the *R.N.S.*, and George, the hero of an apocalyptic work. Wanting to be both creator and participant, he is ripe to appreciate (and create?) George's "herodomcy": "One yearns to make a voyage. Why is one not a hero? I read *The Revised New Syllabus*. Do you likewise, gentlemen and ladies in whose hands this letter is!" (xxx) Here, as in the "Posttape" and "Postscript to the Posttape," Barth juggles his boundaries to undercut any potentially extractable statement.

Science (Eblis Eierkopf and his egg), politics (Peter Greene, the American, and Nikolai, the Russian), and philosophical systems are also brought into and played with in Barth's game sphere. The whole history of Western philosophy is rewritten in the scene in which George Giles listens to Harold Bray's taped lecture. Barth brings this telescoped overview of philosophy to a head in the following diagram (407) out of which George tries to make some sense:

"There is one way to raise a cow"			
Expletivism ("There is [only] one way . . .")		*Adverbialism* ("There [before you] is only one way [of several possible ways] . . .")	
Metaphysical Monism, or *Monistic Expletivism* (". . .[in as much as a unity transcends the apparent diversity] . . .")	*Valuational Monism,* or *Pluralistic Expletivism* (". . . only one way to raise a cow [correctly] . . .")	*Equipollent Pluralism,* or *Pluralistic Adverbialism* (". . . [all equally satisfactory] . . .")	*Disquiparent Pluralism,* or *Hierarchical Adverbialism* (". . . [not equally satisfactory] . . .")

Further gradations occur, with the overall effect affirming Derrida's maxim: In the beginning is hermeneutics; that is, one can only interpret words, then interpret that interpretation, etc. Every sentence, even one as seemingly simple as "There is one way to raise a cow," can be read differently, divided and subdivided into various categories. Philosophers, so this parodic excerpt reveals, can only argue themselves into subtler and subtler positions; they cannot satisfactorily explain what lies behind or outside of language.

The word that probably occurs most frequently in *Giles Goat-Boy* is "answers." Surely, in a novel this long, saturated with divine and tragic heroes, answers have to be provided. Well, they are . . . but, again, only as various interpretive strategies, as various conceptualizations, various fictions. In *Giles Goat-Boy* Barth takes the most serious and valued answers about the nature of reality and the meaning of existence that have been advanced in the Western world and plays with them until they appear as what for Barth they indubitably are—constructs.

Barth plays with the limitations of meaning by turning the riddle of the sphinxes into *The Riddle of the Sphincters* in *Giles Goat-Boy*. Constructing meaning, turning the world into an explicit, meaning-laden place—these are activities that Barth means to parody here and elsewhere. The second sentence of the novel, which is part of a fake "Publisher's Disclaimer," asks the reader "to believe in the sincerity and authenticity of this preface, affirming in return his prerogative to be skeptical of all that follows it" (ix). Anyone acceding to this request must believe that the sentence, "There is one way to raise a cow," has a clear, singular meaning.

Notes

1. John J. Enck, "John Barth: An Interview," *Wisconsin Studies in Contemporary Literature* 6 (1965): 6.

2. David Morrell, *John Barth: An Introduction* (University Park: Pennsylvania State University Press, 1976) 67.

3. John Barth, *The Friday Book: Essays and Other Nonfiction* (New York: Putnam, 1984) 42.

4. Robert Scholes, *The Fabulators* (New York: Oxford University Press, 1967) 163; and Charles B. Harris, *Passionate Virtuosity: The Fiction of John Barth* (Urbana: University of Illinois Press, 1983) 87–88.

5. Jac Tharpe, *John Barth: The Comic Sublimity of Paradox* (Carbondale: Southern Illinois University Press, 1974) 54–55.

6. James T. Gresham, "*Giles Goat-Boy*: Satyr, Satire, and Tragedy Twined," *Genre* 7 (March 1974): 148–63.

7. Northrop Frye, *Anatomy of Criticism* (Princeton: Princeton University Press, 1957), separates the divine and the demonic by these groupings.

8. Mircea Eliade, *The Myth of the Eternal Return* (New York: Pantheon Books, 1965) 16.

9. John Barth, *Giles Goat-Boy* (New York: Doubleday, 1966) 670. Further references will be noted parenthetically in the text.

10. J. E. Cirlot, *A Dictionary of Symbols* (London: Routledge & Kegan Paul, 1962) 140.

CHAPTER SIX

Lost in the Funhouse

*T*he *Floating Opera* and *The End of the Road* attracted a broad base of readers, including those who enjoyed familiar, realistic conventions governing setting, plot, and characterization as well as those who preferred novels of ideas—philosophical inquiries into existentialism and nihilism. Although *The Sot-Weed Factor* and *Giles Goat-Boy* were Barth's first books to depart from this predominantly realistic format, *Lost in the Funhouse* and *Chimera* did so in an even more distinctly experimental way. Those who had found Barth's first two books easy to read and master, to be "readerly" texts in Roland Barthes's words, discovered new and often discomfiting qualities in *Lost in the Funhouse* and *Chimera*. His texts had become "writerly," not easily assimilated, mastered, and consumed; they played language games in ways that kept the text fresh but always difficult.

Probably the most relentlessly experimental of his works, *Lost in the Funhouse* and *Chimera* are, paradoxically, often Barth's most popular. Possibly because of their relative brevity, but most likely because of the raptly

UNDERSTANDING JOHN BARTH

suspenseful nature of the accounts, they ensnare readers who like both taut thrillers and self-scrutinizing methods. The books are also engaging because the short pieces are collected into an integrated series. Whether a spermatozoon fulfills its quest, or Bellerophon achieves his self-definition, or Dunyazade triumphs in her storytelling—these may not sound like the makings of absorbing fiction (especially since they are told with many sets of quotation marks to indicate multiple tellers in a confined space)—nonetheless, these accounts succeed, no doubt because of the way they offer, and yet qualify, tried and true tales.

Lost in the Funhouse: Fiction for Print, Tape, Live Voice, a series of fourteen stories, is fundamentally about telling and listening to stories. As Alfred Appel, Jr., observes, "it is a cerebral, hard-surfaced, often fantastic fiction, whose forms evolve constantly in unexpected, quantum-quick ways."[1] However delightful this experiment, Barth showed some uneasiness about his new style when the book appeared in 1968. Though he had previously published several of these stories in journals, as early as 1963, the collection showed a much different side to Barth's work than the previous novels and might, therefore, have seemed to warrant some defense. The dust jacket of the first edition warns the readers about the experimentation and provides an apologia. In this apologia, taken from an interview at McGill University, Barth says:

LOST IN THE FUNHOUSE

I've been trying to compose pieces which will be quite short, which will have to be published finally in a volume because they'll take some of their resonance from each other—but of which most won't really be designed for the printed page at all. These are experimental pieces . . . [but are not] cold exercises in technique. My feeling about technique in art is that it has about the same value as technique in love-making. That is to say, heartfelt ineptitude has its appeal and so does heartless skill; but what you want is passionate virtuosity.

Although many of these stories have similar modes of presentation and characters, their relation to one another is more difficult to establish, because they do not follow a linear development, and because Barth tries to frustrate the tendency to put ideas and methods into neatly unified patterns. Some deal with the growth of heroes, and some explore the development of techniques and processes of fiction. Although all of Barth's books deal with the way people perceive and articulate experience, *Lost in the Funhouse* is the first that self-consciously treats the communication act so explicitly. Stories that deal with questions of love, heroism, identity, maturation, and war and peace are also self-consciously about narration, structural forms, and audience reception.

Those critics who explore content include Beverly Gray Bienstock, Harold Farwell, Charles B. Harris, and Edgar H. Knapp. Bienstock writes about the book as a search for "one's identity amidst the tangled skeins of past, present, and future."[2] Farwell discusses Barth's vision of absurd love: "Love is not," he says, "something we can create or preserve in opposition to a world gone mad, but . . . the image of that world and its absurdity."[3] Harris explores the relationship between sexuality and language.[4] Knapp takes a more comprehensive view, using the title story to illustrate that Barth plays with nineteenth-century conceptions of mankind, myth, and artistry.[5]

Michael Hinden, Heide Ziegler, and E. P. Walkiewicz are among those who focus on structure and technique. Hinden argues that the book "examines the depletion of certain forms of modernist expression [especially Joyce] and the unbearable self-consciousness of intellectual life."[6] Ziegler thinks that the book is about the writer and the act of writing. To her the volume's primary purpose is structural: "to dissolve genre, narrative mode, authorial voice, and consecutive time sequence."[7] Walkiewicz sees the book as about literary cycles, and he buttresses his view by reference to Douglas R. Hofstadter's study, *Gödel, Escher, Bach: An Eternal Golden Band*.[8] This connection is fascinating, for Hofstadter says of loops: "Implicit in the concept of Strange Loops is the concept of infinity, since what else is a loop but a way of representing an endless process in a finite way."[9] The infinite within the finite is an idea that Barth has explored since *Giles Goat-Boy*.

In the infinite, looping universe of this text, four of the initial stories, set in tidewater Maryland in 1943 and

LOST IN THE FUNHOUSE

the years following, are conventional treatments of the growth of Ambrose Mensch, the protagonist, from sperm to budding author. These include "Night-Sea Journey," "Ambrose His Mark," "Water-Message," and "Lost in the Funhouse"; but "Frame-Tale" and "Petition" are also relevant. Several of the middle stories, which deal with the middle period of life, treat the development of fiction; fiction, itself, is the hero of these tales. These stories include "Echo," "Glossolalia," "Two Meditations," "Autobiography: *A Self-Recorded Fiction*," "Title," and "Life-Story." The terminal stories, paradoxically dealing with the later middle stages of the heroes' lives and the beginning stages of their fiction, return to more realistically drawn characters and situations, drawn from Greek myth, *The Iliad*, and *The Odyssey*. These stories explore the origins of heroic models and storytelling, and include "Menelaiad," and "Anonymiad." In acknowledging the roots of literature Barth also refers to Joyce's *Ulysses*, which has stamped the modern use of classical tradition with its imprint. Together, the stories in this series explore the ways in which fiction and heroes are at once fresh and new as well as traditional and old. They are primarily about the ways in which human experience and literary technique are both like and unlike those preceding them. Nothing is ever wholly the same; nothing is completely different. Life *almost* repeats life; art *almost* repeats art; and life and art *almost* repeat each other.

One of the ways art and life almost repeat one another is through their structural sequences. In the Aristotelian literary scheme, fiction has beginnings, middles, and ends, and for Freitag, following this model, the introduction, rising action, and resolution take the shape of a triangle. Ambrose's discussion of these concepts in "Lost in the Funhouse" reminds the readers of the importance of such views on plot development and structure and helps to situate the rest of the stories, for this book is, like *Chimera*, a more-or-less three-sectioned creature, an image reinforced by the central birthmark of the headless, upside-down bee in "Ambrose His Mark." But, just as Ambrose's bee is truncated, so this book tends to dwell on beginnings and middles; the endings are either beginnings (the optimistic view) or total collapses (the pessimistic view).

Beginnings are central to the first stories of *Lost in the Funhouse*. Taken together, these stories constitute a kind of novella in the classic tradition of the *bildungsroman*, or initiation and growth of the hero. And, since Ambrose is, *LETTERS* confirms, the author of the entire book, each tale can also be understood as fiction about the development of an artist.

In the first of these tales, "Night-Sea Journey," the fundamental human dilemma is laid bare through the dramatic monologue of a sperm, vigorously swimming toward an unknown goal. The arrival, in the story's conclusion, of the sperm at its goal presumably accounts for the conceiving of Ambrose. As the swimming sperm strokes along, he wonders why he is adrift in a sea of other swimmers who seem better equipped than he to deal with the rigors of the night-sea journey. Philosophical in nature, he asks himself the hard questions of life, those that Ambrose later asks: Is there a Maker? Who is he, and what are his nature and motives? Are his intentions benevolent or malevolent? What is the final goal, and how is it attained? Why does one creature succeed and the rest expire? These questions, which are germane to the existence of every thinking being, are given a distinctly humorous cast as they relate to the act of procreation. When readers recognize that the story is about the act of conception, the sperm's other questions become especially meaningful: Did the Maker release the sperm intentionally or inadvertently? Did he want to prevent the sperm from reaching the shore or assist it? Was the Maker "stupid, malicious, insensible, perverse, or asleep and dreaming?"[10] Was the act moral or obscene? Are the swimmers important in themselves or only as they assure the Maker's immortality? The sperm's philosophical sense of the absurd is accentuated by his literary imagination. When he laments, "I have seen the best swimmers of my generation go under. Numberless the number of the dead!" (4) or "Ours not to stop and think; ours but to swim and sink" (5), he invokes Ginsberg, Conrad, and Tennyson. Barth's word play on "Maker" as God, sexual adventurer, and author is beautifully executed and helps the readers to see the various overlapping patterns in the book; it also helps the readers to understand that all such patterns are the product of the human ability to create fictions.

"Ambrose His Mark" extends this discussion of the origins and purposes of life, especially with regard to Ambrose and his family—his bawdy and flirtatious mother Andrea; his conniving, unscrupulous Grandfather Mensch who uses Andrea's fecundity to attract a swarm of bees; the pedantic Uncle Konrad and simple Aunt Rosa who register embarrassment over Andrea's sensuality; and his brother Peter, for whom he feels affection and competition. This story deals with Ambrose's birth and naming as well as his familial and social infrastructure. Konrad's "discourse upon the prophetic aspect of swarming among various peoples" (22) is a key to the story and the collection overall, for it presents the many ways that this infrastructure can be interpreted. His comment illustrates the view that everything is open to acts of interpretation. Few things, if any, can be regarded as neutral. Certainly, Ambrose's "mark" is not one that escapes such cultural scrutiny. The mark is, first of all, his birthmark, and the family members attempt to read it the way others might a Rorschach test. The mark is more a blob than an explicit picture, but Andrea finally declares it to be a three-sectioned, upside-down, headless bee in flight. She draws this conclusion because of the bees swarming when she is breastfeeding Ambrose. The "mark" is also Ambrose's name or signature; but since he is called many names, including Christine, Honey, and Ambrose, since he is not baptized or given his Christian name until the age of thirteen, and since the identity of his father is not certain his name and identity are decidedly questionable. Then, too, the "mark" can be linguistically considered. A mark within structuralist linguistic theory indicates the significant difference between any two meaningful sounds or signs in a given language system. Ambrose is marked or different from other members of his family, though he shares certain characteristics with them.

His marking will continue to change: When Ambrose is weaned, when he begins to make decisions for himself, when in "Water-Message" he finds the message in the bottle on the beach, or when in "Lost in the Funhouse" he gets lost and decides to be an operator of funhouses rather than a player or lover, his identity shifts and changes. These alterations indicate the fluid and indeterminate nature of meaning: Identity is not static, and nothing can ever be interpreted precisely the same from person to person or time to time.

Something that is open to interpretation is language, and young Ambrose is fascinated with words and perplexed about their various meanings. "Water Message" and "Lost in the Funhouse" are primarily about this developing interest. Words represent knowledge for Ambrose; to understand words is to comprehend life. He is drawn to words that seem unusual or elicit unusual responses, words like "facts" and "facts of life," which may be used to indicate factual knowledge or sexual mysteries, or metaphorical phrases like "lump in the throat" or "breaking out in a cold sweat" that describe his adolescent feelings. The very sound of words attracts him, but more than that, he is interested in words in relation to the values of his changing milieu and the way in which literature affects attitudes. When he finds the "water-message" in the bottle, it represents a special act of communication and knowledge to which only he is privy.

As a child in the fourth grade ("Water-Message"), he is undersized and studious, the target of the bullies in the school, but he has a vivid sense of language and a rich literary imagination. He thinks of the twin terrors of his neighborhood, the Spitz dog and Crazy Alice, as Scylla and Charybdis, names that he chose from *The Book of Knowledge*. He names the boys' club the Occult Order of the Sphinx, though he is considered too young to join it. He wants to be initiated into the whispered mysteries that the older boys seem to understand, the reason for their laughing about what Peggy Robbins did with Tommy James at the clubhouse. Chagrined to be cowardly, young, and excluded from the discourse of the older boys, he dreams a literary dream of heroism, rescuing Peggy Robbins from distress, loving and forgiving her for her indiscretion and unfaithfulness, and, putting aside his personal dislike of Wimpy Jones, saving him too. He thinks of Peggy as his courtly love, and he describes her in the most conventional romantic language.

Ambrose's choice of vocabulary, and hence percep-

LOST IN THE FUNHOUSE

tion, is influenced by what he reads. When he describes his encounters with childhood rivals and potential sweethearts as "Odysseus steering under anvil clouds" (45) or thinks of himself as slashing his "way under portcullis and over moat, it was lay about with mace and halberd" (46), when he wants access to the boys' club, the Occult Order of the Sphinx—he has brought Odysseus, King Arthur, and Huck Finn into a working relationship with his contemporary existence. These fictions influence the way Ambrose thinks about himself and reality; they inform his vision, mold his thoughts, and direct his emotions. In Barth's terms life does imitate art, not just in the sense that certain events resemble those described in art, but also in the sense that the concepts of fiction really do influence or "contaminate" our view of events.

Because perceptions are governed by words and cultural constructions, descriptions tend to be recycled endlessly, but always with some differences. The title story, "Lost in the Funhouse," especially stresses the function of repetition and distortion, sameness and difference. The story concerns the thirteen-year-old Ambrose, taken on an Independence Day holiday to Ocean City. With him are his mother, father, and Uncle Karl, as well as his fifteen-year-old brother Peter and fourteen-year-old Magda G——, whom both brothers fancy. The story details the ride to the beach, Ambrose's discovery of raw sexuality under the boardwalk, the teenagers' foray into the funhouse with its peculiar distorting mirrors, and Ambrose's getting lost. The story, written in strained, self-conscious, third-person prose, conveys Ambrose's increasing awareness that all expression is learned and hence sufficiently alien. He is also aware that his developing sexuality is estranging—part of him, but not one with him. He recognizes that he is like other youths in his developing sexual awareness and desires, but he thinks of himself as a less confident and able lover than his brother Peter or the anonymous sailor in the funhouse. At the same time, he realizes that, while all his family and acquaintances speak the English language, he has more facility with it and more interest in the conventions of literature. Both sex and language are, consequently, "natural" and estranging. This same-different, conformity-alienation pattern is visually presented in the image of the funhouse mirrors. These mirrors give back a reflection to the viewer, but that reflection is a one-dimensional imitation and not the original. Moreover, in a funhouse the glass itself is distorting—shortening, broadening, or elongating the viewer, so that repetition differs more than usual. Life and art, Ambrose and the funhouse of fiction, do repeat socially and literarily established images and patterns, but they also change and distort them.

Appropriately, the more style-oriented stories reflect similar concerns. The first story, "Frame-Tale," is also about repetition, but primarily the codified or repetitive introductions to tales. "Once Upon a Time" and "There Was a Story That Began" are two such formulaic beginnings, which, when combined, suggest the unending "beginningness" of stories. This device not only suggests that literature depends upon patterns of repetition but, in inviting the reader to cut, twist, and link the ends, emphasizes that no form perfectly reduplicates its predecessor. As the lead story in the collection, "Frame-Tale" establishes the book's commitment, not to content or realism and all its conventional accoutrements, but to form itself.

In its distinctly gothic, nonrealistic presentation, "Petition" also establishes the importance of repetition and emphasizes the notion of "sameness" and "difference." The story deals with the written petition to a visiting dignitary, Prajadhipok, that he assist in separating the narrator, an unnamed Siamese twin, from his brother. The narrator has become increasingly burdened with the behavior of his brother to the point that he wants a radical solution. "Fastened front to rear," the Siamese twins are the same: sharing the same life blood and muscle tissue, they are unenduringly part-and-parcel of each other. But they are also different. One is earthy, sensual, bawdy, gregarious, realistic, and vocal; the other (the narrator-writer) is cerebral, solitary, romantic, and unable to speak. Although the narrator is aware of their differences, he seems unable to cope with his dilemma: "I affirm our difference—all the difference in the world!— but have endeavored in vain to work out with him a reasonable cohabitation" (62). The narrator cannot abide being both identical and different: "To be one: paradise! To be two: bliss! But to be both and neither is unspeakable" (71). In terms of form, to follow in the tradition of renowned masterpieces is preferable; to be completely new and original is acceptable; but to be both new and repetitive, to be the twist in a loop, is intolerable. Presented within the imagery of twinship and doubleness, the story is, in certain respects, about the artist's difficulty in trying to adhere to tradition and break from it. These tales all stress the beginnings of life and fiction. No beginning or birth can be seen as a wholly unique event, for each duplicates existing patterns and species. Yet, each beginning, however repetitive, is also in some significant way unique. To recognize this combination allows one (self or story) to get on with the plot.

The stories that constitute the second section of the book, the middle period of life and "rising action" literature, are those beginning with "Echo." These are the most difficult tales exploring lives and styles of writing which, like a needle caught in the groove of a record, seem trapped in predictable responses and patterns or doomed to failure. As the title suggests, "Echo" is a variant of the Narcissus legend, told here not only from the female perspective but one that centers on Echo's storytelling abilities. Beginning with the gift of divine narrative, telling lively stories of her own fabricating, Echo is condemned by "the Queen of heaven" to repeat the voices of others. Her repetition is echoed by others within the tale—Narcissus who falls in love with his reflection in the spring of Donacon and Tiresias who has lived so long, heard so many stories, and given so much advice that he can no longer keep one separate from another. Such apparently mechanical repetitions do not, however, lead to identical meanings or conclusions, for as the narration affirms, "A cure for self-absorption is saturation: telling the story over as though it were another's until like a much-repeated word it loses sense" (98). Repetitive excess can lead to a different message from the original; excessive repetition undermines origins. But not all repetition leads to excess. Echo, for instance, "never, as popularly held, repeats all, like gossip or mirror. She edits, heightens, mutes, turns others' words to her end" (100). She is a writer, echoing previously written works, but always choosing words offered by her culture to create new fiction. Her echo is both a tribute to and a distortion of the originals. Her response prolongs her life and storytelling, whereas Narcissus dies in his attempts to embrace his reflection and to perpetuate what is intimately known and familiar.

Although the first stories raise questions about the individual speaker/writer in relation to communication codes, certain middle stories ("Title" and "Life-Story") decry the apparent falseness and staleness of overused patterns: "Beginning: in the middle, past the middle, nearer three-quarters done, waiting for the end. Consider how dreadful so far: passionlessness, abstraction, pro, dis. And it will get worse. Can we possibly continue?" (105). In "Title" the narrative becomes its own narrator, lamenting its literary conventions, hating the

medium in which it is told. It recognizes its similarity
to other stories and feels crippled by its lack of individuality and spontaneity. By having the stories describe
their own frustration and weaknesses, Barth emphasizes his central working premise: Words and literary
patterns are so common that the idea of going beyond
them to new beginnings often seems impossible. Since
speakers can only use language generally available and
commonly understood, and since previous literary works
provide the basis of all further writing, an author/narrator/
story may quite legitimately feel that everything has been
said before, an attitude that can preclude further writing: "What now. Everything's been said already, over
and over; I'm as sick of this as you are; there's nothing
to say. Say nothing" (105). Notions of growth and progress, both on human and literary levels, give way to
exhaustion, resignation, and ultimately, despair. Instead
of prolonging life or the text, repetition may lead to
blankness of vision and a lack of stirring vitality, and for
the writer this awareness leads to another blankness: a
failure to put anything at all on the page. Self-consciousness about the failure of vision and writing as a result
of disillusionment following youthful romanticism can
lead to emotional and textual breakdown. The distressed
narrator of "Title" says it well: "We're more than half-
way through, as I remarked at the outset: youthful vigor,
innocent exposition, positive rising action—all that is
behind us. . . . In this dehuman, exhausted, ultimate ad-
jective hour, . . . every humane value has become un-

tenable, and not only love, decency, and beauty but even compassion and intelligibility are no more than one or two subjective complements to complete the sentence . . ." (107). Unable to finish his penultimate sentence, the narrator still hopes that self-consciousness can be used against itself in order "to turn ultimacy against itself to make something new and valid, the essence whereof would be the impossibility of making something new" (109).

"Life-Story" is also about the seeming impossibility of individuality, but this latter tale is not self-engendered, as "Title" claims to be; it has an author, whose life the reader learns about. This author laments his own self-consciousness and bemoans his birth in the age of modernism rather than in a period that valued heroism and heroic rhetoric, that is, a "conservative, 'realistic,' unself-conscious" style with "arresting circumstance, bold character, trenchant action" (116, 118). Because he is a product of his age, his style slips into the "self-conscious, vertiginously arch, fashionably solipsistic, [and] unoriginal" (117). He begins to wonder if the world is not itself a novel and he a character, or he himself a fiction with thoughts that are also fictions. In that event, his story becomes a frame-tale of a story within a story. Ultimately, this narrator cannot discover what is real and what is fabricated or what he wills and what is willed for him. Unable to control his style and content he is lost in the funhouse of fiction as much as Ambrose, but, in the middle period of his life, with fewer resources. Instead of believing he is in control, he has to accept the likelihood that he is controlled, that he is someone else's fiction, and that he has no other identity. Ironically, in talking about his problems in writing, the author-narrator fashions a story about the impossibility of fashioning a story.

The last two stories in the series concern the late middle years of the characters' lives, but not old age. There is no final or grand conclusion to these stories, for as in "Lost in the Funhouse" and "Life-Story," a crisis or end also marks a beginning. These last two stories are set in the ancient Greece of Odysseus and Penelope, Menelaus and Helen, and Agamemnon and Clytemnestra. These tales do not concern the glories of the battles, but rather the origins of storytelling. Menelaus, the narrator of the "Menelaiad," has come back from the Trojan Wars and is living his later years at home with Helen, visited on this particular evening by Telemachus, the disguised son of Odysseus. As a means of keeping Telemachus from sleeping with the still beautiful Helen, Menelaus keeps him by the fire with his stories. He begins his storytelling by describing their present circumstances but then tells of past conversations, which are placed in separate quotation marks, each set moving the reader ever further from the verifiable present. As he describes past events and conversations, Menelaus fears that he is only a narrating voice without any substantial identity: "One thing's certain:

somewhere Menelaus lost course and steersman, went off track, never got back on, lost hold of himself, became a record merely, the record of his loosening grasp. He's the story of his life, with which he ambushes the unwary unawares" (131). What Menelaus grapples with is that the essence of each person is only his or her story. Telemachus is not a real visitor, trying to bed Helen, but only a voice, responding to Menelaus's and Helen's. Despite her great sexual appeal, the allure of Helen is mainly her words. Her perplexing statement that she loves Menelaus undoes him for years until Proteus advises him to "beg Love's pardon for your want of faith. Helen chose you without reason because she loves you without cause; embrace her without question and watch your weather change" (161). Each person has a narrative that intersects with other narratives, but the reality, the truth, at the bottom of these narratives is impossible to locate. The quotations within quotations stress that there is no guarantee of meaning from the act of speech; there is no center or locus of meaning, and life has to be lived in spite of that knowledge.

The narrator of the penultimate story is also left only with words. Paid to be a minstrel in Agamemnon's court, he stays there while the warriors go off to the Trojan Wars. While the others are absent, he is charged by Agamemnon with observing Clytemnestra to make certain that she remains faithful. Clytemnestra and her lover Aegisthus, however, arrange to dispose of the poet, and he is tricked into going aboard a ship and abandoned on an uninhabited island. There he writes his works, sending them to sea in empty amphorae.

An innocent minstrel, he was not prepared for the fruits of his introduction to court life, and too late he discovered that his minstrelsy inflamed the passions of Clytemnestra and Aegisthus. His political responsibility of spying on Clytemnestra in order to prevent her infidelity and his artistic mission of telling interesting stories that calm the passions are completely undermined, and he is exiled. In exile, he finds his art growing, though he has few resources—nine amphorae of wine, squid ink, and his pen, and no papyrus except for the skin of the goats he butchers.

Since he has not been allowed to live out the rest of his life in society, he begins his writing "in the middle— where too I'll end, there being alas to my arrested history as yet no denouement" (169). He later concludes, "there's no denouement, only a termination or ironical coda" (200). He has only memories of a once-active court life: "Merope's love, Helen's whoring, Menelaus's noise, Agamemnon's slicing up his daughter for the weatherman—all the large and deadly passions of men and women, wolves, frogs, nightingales; all this business of seizing life, grabbing hold with both hands . . ." (171). In isolation, he plans great works of art—his own life story, the Trojan wars, Agamemnon's court, and Clytemnestra's infidelity. He writes these in many genres, but his last, the one before the goatskin runs out, is to be his life story in nine parts. These intentions are never quite realized. The nine parts are not perfectly executed. He has a part called "1 1/2," and "3" does not exist, for he says, "Three, my crux, my core, I'm cutting you out; ———; there, at the heart, never to be filled, a mere lacuna" (183).

Despite Anonymous's discouragement that he cannot fulfill his intentions and that the manuscript has not gone as he hoped, despite his feelings of defeat and exhaustion, and despite his view that no one will probably ever read his manuscripts, he does accomplish something. His writing saves him from suicide. Had he not been able to "tell" (though to no certain audience), he would have been bereft of hope. No matter how amateurish, decayed, or incomplete the work of art, it functions to save the author and, potentially, the reader. By a remote chance his works may communicate something to someone. Dubious whether his amphorae stuffed with manuscripts will ever reach an audience, he himself finds a jar washed up on his own beach. Whether his own or another's he does not know, but he does not care: "Now I began to imagine that the world contained another like myself. Indeed, it might be astrew with isled souls, become minstrels perforce, and the sea a-clink with literature! Alternatively, one or several of my messages may have got through." He then adds, "I never ceased to allow the likelihood that the indecipherable ciphers were my own; that the sea had fertilized me as it were with my own seed. No matter, the principle was the same: that I could be thus messaged, even by that stranger my former self" (196). An artist can be "messaged" by his or her own work; communication between past and present or between persons can exist. Literature does have a function, and the communication act does not have to be aborted, though the message may be somewhat misunderstood. These concluding stories do not affirm heroic endings and structured documents, but they affirm the possibility of new beginnings and new cycles. They suggest that living and writing, while repetitive and without individuality, may still have purpose, however apparently undiscoverable.

These new cycles and patterns of repetition depend fully upon the relationship between author, text, and reader or what Barth calls teller, tale, and told. *Lost in the Funhouse* rejects a belief in the author as a genius, one who with divine intuition creates a work beyond the abilities of more common human beings. Rather, Barth advances the view that writing is hard work, with the artists never fully in control and with no divine reassurance or insight behind them. The unpredictability of writing is further complicated by the role of the reader, who the narrator of "Life-Story" calls "you, dogged, uninsultable, print-oriented bastard" (127). If potential readers refuse to read the work, then it dies, regardless of the intrinsic merit of the text itself. The narrator of "Life Story" argues that a story cannot even commit suicide without the reader's decision to close the book. "You who listen give me life in a manner of speaking" (35). Although a story may be conceived by the author, if it remains unread, its life is aborted. Readers have considerable independence and bring certain attitudes and understandings to bear on the text, so that the author's intentions, if ever known, are never wholly fulfilled. Meaning and immortality of the text are generated by both author and reader, text and interpreter. The message the author intends may be perceived quite differently by readers who have their own concerns and structures. Acts of reading, however repetitive, are always different, as are acts of writing. The writer and reader together create the text. Like an infinite loop, the interaction of text and reader seems always open to new possibilities, but insofar as the text itself is finite, the possibilities are not truly infinite.

Notes

1. Alfred Appel, Jr., "The Art of Artifice," *The Nation* 207 (28 Oct. 1968): 441.

2. Beverly Gray Bienstock, "Lingering on the Autognostic Verge: John Barth's *Lost in the Funhouse*," *Modern Fiction Studies* 19 (Spring 1973): 70.

3. Harold Farwell, "John Barth's Tenuous Affirmation: 'The Absurd, Unending Possibility of Love,'" *Georgia Review* 28 (Summer 1974): 290–306.

4. Charles B. Harris, *Passionate Virtuosity: The Fiction of John Barth* (Urbana: University of Illinois Press, 1983) 106.

5. Edgar H. Knapp, "Found in the Barthhouse: Novelist as Savior," *Modern Fiction Studies* 14 (Winter 1968–69): 446–53.

6. Michael Hinden, "*Lost in the Funhouse:* Barth's Use of the Recent Past," *Twentieth Century Literature* 19 (Jan.–Oct. 1973): 108.

7. Heide Ziegler, *John Barth* (London: Methuen, 1987) 50.

8. E. P. Walkiewicz, *John Barth* (Boston: Twayne, 1986) 84–109.

9. Douglas R. Hofstadter, *Gödel, Escher, Bach: An Eternal Golden Band* (New York: Vintage Books, 1980) 15.

10. John Barth, *Lost in the Funhouse: Fiction for Print, Tape, Live Voice* (Garden City, N.Y.: Doubleday, 1968) 7. Further references will be noted parenthetically in the text.

CHAPTER SEVEN

Chimera

Neither a collection of short stories nor a traditional novel, *Chimera* (1972) stands out as an entity as oddly shaped as the mythical beast, chimera. That "animal" is a tripartite being, a fire-breathing monster that has a lion's head, a goat's body, and a serpent's tail. Similarly, *Chimera* contains three parts of varying proportions and seemingly disparate qualities. The first section, "Dunyazadiad," which uses the characters and motifs from *The Thousand and One Nights*, is approximately fifty pages in length. The second section, "Perseid," approximately fifty percent longer than "Dunyazadiad," shifts the focus to Greek mythology. The third section, "Bellerophoniad," approximately fifty percent longer than the other two sections combined, relates to "Perseid" much more than to "Dunyazadiad," for Bellerophon knows of his cousin Perseus's deeds and aspires to like status. The only explicit connection "Bellerophoniad" has with the first section is the mention of the "gynocrats," the Amazons who are a distinct society of women. "Perseid" has no direct connections with "Dunyazadiad."

Barth provides an incremental structure in *Chimera;* an overview, though, does not immediately divulge any unifying shape or rhythm in the book. Indeed, *Chimera* often gives the appearance of being a chimera, which, in common parlance, means a fancy or a whim. Nonetheless, this odd beast works, in part because each section is concerned with the act of telling and listening to stories and in part because each section deals with this issue in terms of mythology. Just as the chimera is a curiosity, a beast of uncertain parts, the book, *Chimera,* also eludes an easy generic classification.

It should be noted that *Chimera's* shape has been altered from its original state. At first, as David Morell notes, *Chimera* had the following order: "Perseid," "Bellerophoniad," "Dunyazadiad." An editor at Random House suggested that "Dunyazadiad" be placed first, "Perseid" second, and "Bellerophoniad" third because "Dunyazadiad" was, for her, the most accessible of the three. Barth, after some reluctance, agreed to the request.

Critics have been generally more perplexed and divided about *Chimera* than about the rest of the Barthian canon. Some find this book a landmark in its exploration of fictive possibilities. An early reviewer, Jerry H. Bryant, sees it as a forum for the author to investigate the various literary problems the contemporary writer faces in the process of invention.[1] In a similar vein, Heide

Ziegler discusses the way the recycling of myth is used to define the role of the artist: "The postmodernist author can no longer be an authentic artist; his only claim to originality lies in the reflection upon this dilemma from his own point of view."[2] Others see the book in thematically different ways. Charles B. Harris views it as a comment on the patriarchal tradition in religion, myth, and writing: "Each of the three myths Barth includes in *Chimera* records in some fashion the demise of the matriarchy and the consciousness with which it is associated."[3] David Morrell and E. P. Walkiewicz both emphasize the logarithmic spiral form implicit in the structure and content of the tales. Walkiewicz views this form as "the offspring of mixed parents, the product of the mating of Fact and Fancy, the Real and Ideal, and an emblem of one of the work's major themes, the chimerical nature of human freedom."[4] Whatever the critics' perception, it is certain that the role of myth and the authorial treatment of it is at the center.

Most twentieth-century works, when they bring mythology, Greek or otherwise, into play, use that material in one of two ways: As a comparison by which the current period is measured against a previous one (such as in "The Waste Land" where the comparison is unflattering to those living in the twentieth century), or as the mythological underpinning for today's more secular doings (such as in *Ulysses* where Leopold Bloom is meant to be a kind of updated Odysseus and Molly Bloom, his wife, a kind of updated Penelope). Rarely does a writer risk what Barth does in *Chimera:* a rewriting of myths directly, featuring Scheherazade, Perseus, and Bellerophon, in their prescribed roles and deeds. The rewriting is done in contemporary prose, with contemporary perspectives and styles. (Perhaps only John Updike in *The Centaur* attempts to sustain such a consistently myth-oriented focus and framework.)

To offer the stories of Scheherazade, Perseus, and Bellerophon, with heroic actions and/or mythic deeds, in a traditional format would be to give contemporary readers something remote from their experience; moreover, there is a sense now that heroism cannot be presented uncorruptedly in an era in which motive is always scrutinized and psychoanalysis flourishes. Irony, which makes interpretation so complex, is worked into *Chimera* so that not only the readers, but also the characters have to debate and speculate about often-narrated classical tales.

While other works by Barth are more extended and densely written (full of lists and an overwhelming array of details), *Chimera* makes special demands on its readers because of the unrelenting number of mythological figures Barth parades through the book. Such minor characters as Glaucus, Aerisius, and Autolycus, as obscure to classicists as they are to general readers, get recycled from the Greek myths into *Chimera*. Only Jerome Bray, who projects a revolutionary novel that is a product of his computer and who also appears with a similar obsession in *LETTERS,* and the Genie, a Barth-like figure who coaches Scheherazade on telling tales from his vantage point of the twentieth century, give *Chimera* any characters who would be familiar to contemporary readers of fiction.

Fusing ancient stories with a self-consciously postmodern authorial presence, Barth manifests his love of traditional stories and their interrelationships and affirms his skepticism regarding the sanctity of those tales. That is, circumstances have altered the way myths are both told and understood. Of his use of mythic material, Barth says the following:

> . . . when you consciously use an old myth, a received myth, like the myth of Perseus, or the myth of Helen, Paris, and Menelaus, then whatever there is of the originally mythopoeic in your own imagination is either going to come in somewhere else in that text—with new characters, or language, or new twists to the old myth, or else will simply flow in to fill in those mythic receptacles which go by the names of Paris, Menelaus, Helen.[5]

Contamination, seen here as a positive term, is thus inescapable for Barth. A figure from mythology becomes his invention whether already well-chronicled or not. Moreover, much of the richness of *Chimera* comes from this awareness: Scheherazade saves herself in the manner told in *The Thousand and One Nights;* Perseus falls in love with Andromeda and beheads Medusa as recounted by Robert Graves in *The Greek Myths;* Bellerophon slays the dragon, Chimera, again as recounted in *The Greek Myths*. Yet, by having the stories told in contemporary voices by multiple narrators, Barth effectively invents different characters who have the names Scheherazade, Perseus, and Bellerophon.

"Dunyazadiad" features characters for whom telling tales is a matter of life and death. Scheherazade's dilemma is that she must entertain King Shahryar so that she can escape the fate of her precursors, virgins who are taken to bed by the King and then killed by him. By masterfully developing the art of narrative, she keeps him longing for a sequel each succeeding night. Barth's twist is to have Dunyazade, Scheherazade's sister, tell her own death-postponing tale to her own listener and potential executioner, Shah Zaman, who happens to be King Shahryar's brother. To produce the story-within-a-story-within-a-story motif, Barth places Dunyazade at the foot of Shahryar's and Scheherazade's bed where she can be a listener—and a viewer—in addition to a teller. The lesson that Dunyazade and Barth's readers ultimately learn is that each listener is both voyeur and creator. The reader passively reads the text and also gives it life.

Complicating the narrative, Barth gives himself a cameo appearance as the Genie who tells Scheherazade and Dunyazade the stories he is reading from *The Thousand and One Nights* that will be used by Scheherazade to captivate the King and spare her life: "He was strange-looking enough: a light-skinned fellow of forty or so,

smooth-shaven and bald as a roc's egg. . . . He was tall
and healthy and pleasant enough in appearance, except
for queer lenses that he wore in a frame over his eyes."[6]
(Barth repeats this pattern again in *The Tidewater Tales*
where Djean, Scheherazade, and Dunyazade are again
brought together.) This scenario allows Barth to indulge
in one of his favorite activities—reader response and
literary criticism in the context of the fiction itself. The
two storytellers, one from an early oral culture and one
from a late postmodern one, examine the relationship
of life and art as well as of form and content: "They
speculated endlessly on such questions as whether a
story might imaginably be framed from inside, as it were,
so that the usual relation between container and contained would be reversed and paradoxically reversible—
and what . . . human state of affairs such an odd construction might usefully figure" (24). Barth has succeeded
in reversing the relation between container and contained—telling the stories to Scheherazade that she in
The Thousand and One Nights tells to him. Moreover, out
of this situation comes the potential for another new
twist to the story. That is, Barth completes his own work
which the Genie had said was a conundrum—how "to
go beyond them [his stories] toward a future they were
not attuned to and, by some magic, at the same time
go back to the original springs of narrative" (10).

Refusing Scheherazade's offer of her body for "his"
stories, the Genie feeds her them because of his admira-
tion for her stature, her own allure as a tale teller for

twentieth-century writers. Although he seems sublimely innocent and unpostmodern about love and marriage, the Genie knows that his storytelling, while not threatening his physical life in any murderous way, does cause problems that those in perhaps more innocent eras did not face. The Genie presents the problem of composition in a self-conscious, tale-saturated world in terms of a snail:

There's a kind of snail in the Maryland marshes—perhaps I invented him—that makes his shell as he goes along out of whatever he comes across, cementing it with his own juices, and at the same time makes his path instinctively toward the best available material for his shell; he carries his history on his back, living in it, adding new and larger spirals to it from the present as he grows. That snail's pace has become my pace—but I'm going in circles, following my own trail! I've quit reading and writing; I've lost track of who I am; my name's just a jumble of letters; so's the whole body of literature; strings of letters and empty spaces, like a code that I've lost the key to. (10–11)

The Genie/Barth finds the key in the treasure, in the completion of his "Dunyazadiad." Just as the sisters utilized him for their tales, he utilizes them for his tale. That tale, "Dunyazadiad," is the model for an entrée by the contemporary, self-conscious author into materials of the past.

As he does in the rewriting of *Oedipus Rex* in *Giles*

Goat-Boy, Barth achieves much of his comedy by attrib-
uting contemporary slang and up-to-date styles to mythic and heroic figures. Scheherazade, for instance, at
the time King Shahryar was ravaging the young women
of his country, was an "undergraduate arts-and-sciences
major at Banu Sasan University" (5). In addition to being "Homecoming Queen, valedictorian-elect, and a four-
letter varsity athlete" (5), she is also a scholar who seeks
in current academic disciplines—political science and
psychology—a way to stop King Shahryar from aug-
menting his count of "deflowered and decapitated Mos-
lem girls" (6). She turns finally to myth and folklore—
more specifically to a genie . . . and genius, that is to the
magic of fiction, Barth's ever-present elixir.

As Scheherazade enunciates the problem, words
are magical, "but the magic words in one story aren't
magical in the next" (7). Moreover, in the phrase that
resonates throughout "Dunyazadiad," "the key to the
treasure is the treasure." In other words, the right story
will not only be the key to the resolution of her dilemma, but will be the treasure itself. Words, language,
are simultaneously key and treasure. What Barth has
done brilliantly in "Dunyazadiad" is to find a way to
renew a treasurable resource, *The Thousand and One Nights*,
and to rewrite subtly and originally an old story. He
does the same with "Perseid" and "Bellerophoniad."

In "Dunyazadiad" *The Thousand and One Nights* is
worked through the two brothers and two sisters of
those tales as well as the Genie. The complexities of

tellers and listeners are enormous and delightful; for instance, the Genie both tells tales to Scheherazade and reads them through her; Dunyazade both tells tales to Shah Zaman and listens to Scheherazade's stories. Thus, the act of telling and listening to stories comes to dominate "Dunyazadiad." The debate that develops centers on different kinds of audiences for storytellers of different eras. As the Genie somewhat wistfully tells it, the only "readers of artful fiction" in the postmodern era are "critics, other writers, and unwilling students who, left to themselves, preferred music and pictures to words" (9).

Artful readers, a minority of readers who are themselves in a minority just by being readers, learn that the pleasures of the text come from its fictiveness and its sensuousness. Fictions, the Genie tells the sisters, are the world's supreme pleasures: Some "were so much more valuable than fact that in rare instances their beauty made them real" (17).

Dunyazade, an apt pupil of the Genie's, is also raptly attentive to the other art Scheherazade is honing. Perched at the foot of Shahryar's bed, she gets lessons in the art of making love. It is a practice that in Barth's terms is richly interwoven with narrative skills. Dunyazade watches as the pleasure of the text gets its graphic, sexual incarnation. Both acts—sexual and narrative—are integrated in "Dunyazadiad." The Genie goes on to develop even further a carnal theory of fiction in which stories-within-stories-within-stories are described in terms of multiple orgasms. "Narrative," the Genie maintains finally, "was a love-relation, not a rape" (26), an attempt to provide a model of harmony that undoes male brutality (Shahryar's multiple raping and Bellerophon's one act of rape, to name two examples), so much a part of the traditional stories Barth is both writing and, especially vis-à-vis patriarchal domination, unwriting. Indeed, the climax (itself, of course, a loaded term) of "Dunyazadiad" contains a reversal of the rapes that King Shahryar has inflicted on Samarkand, his kingdom. It also provides a reversal of the teller-listener relationship in that Shah Zaman, in order to retain his life, tells Dunyazade the story of how he, like his brother, has taken a virgin each night, but instead of killing her has allowed her to flee to a self-sufficient community of women.

"Perseid" begins with the maxim, "Stories last longer than men, stones than stories, stars than stones" (59); of these enduring substances, only stories can be created by human beings. This section of *Chimera* celebrates those three elements that prevail over mere mortals. It chronicles a good many stories, including one about Medusa whose stare "gorgonizes" or turns to stone her targets; the vantage point is that of Perseus and Medusa who have been "estellated," that is, become a constellation of stars. "Perseid" gains in complexity because, as in "Dunyazadiad," there is a mixture of tellers and listeners. The unifying voice of the narration is not at all clear. David Morrell believes it to be Polyeidus in his various shapes, but Charles B. Harris thinks it the Genie.[7] Perseus, Medusa, and Calyxa, a third figure and another lover of Perseus, contaminate the Perseus myth by recounting it, even as Perseus contaminates his own legend by trying to repeat it. Later, Bellerophon contaminates the myth even further by trying to follow its pattern by way of an "autobiographical road map."

The best-known elements of that myth are Perseus's beheading of Medusa, freeing Andromeda who has been pinioned naked to a cliff, and turning the wedding guests to stone with Medusa's severed head. They are translated by Barth into a much more colloquial language than that in which they were originally cast. A doctor, for instance, urges a vacation on Perseus, telling him it will "do you oodles," and he and Andromeda, whom he has married, speak domestically of taking his advice and "parking the kids" (72). A racier-than-the-classical manner of detailing the sexual adventures of mythological figures helps to contextualize the classics; that is, the lofty manner of presenting and also receiving such doings dictates their interpretation. By describing Calyxa's activities as "group-grope, gang-bang, daisy-chain, and other perversions" (74), Barth both demystifies the Greek myths and reveals the late twentieth century's own stylized way of depicting such material.

Despite its jocular and effortless tone, "Perseid" is not easily unwound. As Charles Harris points out,[8] Barth borrows an idea from Virgil's *Aeneid* to allow Perseus to review his life as he sees it represented artistically on the walls of

a marble chamber that unwound from my left-foot cor-
ner in a grand spiral like the triton-shell that Dedalus
threaded for Cocalus, once about the bed and out of
sight. Upon its walls curved graven scenes in low relief,
each half again and more its predecessor's breadth, to
the number of seven where the chamber wound from
view—which scenes . . . I saw depicted alabasterly the
several chapters of my youth. (61)

At forty years of age, the same age as the Genie, Perseus fights to rejuvenate his life by repeating and recon-
sidering the deeds that gained him fame. Despite its
myth-laden nature, "Perseid" can be read as the story
of a mid-life crisis.

By the end of "Perseid" Perseus has, with the coach-
ing of Calyxa, who has chided him for wanting to be
twenty and with Andromeda again, become more at
peace with himself. The desire to replicate earlier deeds
has been displaced by contentment at the retelling of
the story. As Perseus says at the end of his tale, "our
net estate: to have become, like the noted music of our
tongue, those silent, visible signs . . ." (133).

Life and the telling of it, the experience and its
"visible sign"—a doubled perspective is necessary in
reading this novella of Barth's (as well as all his other
works). The ironic tone that infiltrates "Perseid" com-
promises the sublime ending. Aging may provide dis-
tance and detachment, but stasis and silence can
become stagnant. As Medusa says, when she and Per-

seus discuss their situation from the vantage point of the heavens, "Down there our mortal lives are living themselves out, or've long since done—together or apart, comic tragic beautiful ugly" (133). Myths, too, can become stagnant, though any reliving of them, however artificial and self-conscious, rejuvenates them. Barth revivifies his own life at forty and Perseus's life by adding his own voice to the telling of this already told tale.

"Bellerophoniad" is the section of *Chimera* which, because of its length and the intrusion of characters from other Barth fictions, plays most complexly with the notion of recounting and yet altering a myth. "The Pattern of Mythic Heroism" is as incessant a refrain here as "The key to the treasure is the treasure" in "Dunyazadiad." Bellerophon, like a character in search of an author, insists on forcing his life into that heroic pattern and into the demands of being a demigod:

Bellerophon believes (echoing for a moment, if lamely, the prancing rhythms and alliterations of the *Perseid*) . . . it was [Polyeidus] who showed Bellerus as a boy the Pattern of Mythic Heroism, fourth quadrant of which calls for the mature hero's sudden and mysterious fall from the favor of gods and men; his departure, voluntary or otherwise, from the city of his own establishment; his mysterious apotheosis on a hilltop, symbolic counterpart of the place of his divine conception; et cetera. (140–141)

CHIMERA

Bellerophon leaves his own family and prosperous kingdom to promote himself as a hero, meeting the requirement of the Pattern.

Barth quotes a large part of Graves's chapter on Bellerophon in *The Greek Myths* to provide the external classical measure by which Bellerophon judges himself and others evaluate him. What Barth does, again through multiple voices, including that of Polyeidus, described as a shape-shifter and a metaphor for the protean and manipulating artist, is offer all the details of Graves, but give them in such a context that Bellerophon becomes different from traditional accounts. To his wife, his Amazon lover, and the reader, Bellerophon tells in his own way—or rather in Barth's way—his own tales: how he rode Pegasus, killed the Chimera, and stabbed the Medusa.

Polyeidus, being introduced as another voice and thereby complicating matters, can provide not the polished sheen of a classical account of his life, but only a postmodern, tenuous mythification: "What I *might* manage . . . is to turn *myself* from this interview into you-in-*Bellerophoniad*-form: a certain number of printed pages in a language not untouched by Greek, to be read by a limited number of 'Americans,' not all of whom will finish or enjoy them" (307). Bellerophon rails against such a limited canonization, complaining that "It's not at all what I had in mind for Bellerophon. It's a beastly fiction, ill-proportioned, full of longueurs, lumps, lacunae, a kind of monstrous mixed metaphor" (308). In short it's a chimera, which is all postmodern fiction can be, unless it offers ironically an organic, unified whole. Questions of, and scholarly inquiries into, the mythic hero are more prominent in "Bellerophoniad" than the doings of Bellerophon. In parodic, yet incisive, critical commentary, Barth reveals how reviewers of *The Sot-Weed Factor* found the heroic pattern traced in Joseph Campbell's *The Hero with a Thousand Faces* to be central to that book. Only after their comments, Barth claims, did he examine the scholarship and deploy it in later books.

"Bellerophoniad" anticipates the self-reflexive material of *LETTERS*. Barth appears, not in the cameo role of the Genie, but more complexly via material from his other works of fiction. Excerpts from *Lost in the Funhouse* are recycled. Also, a seduction scene in "Bellerophoniad" is nearly identical with that between Jake and Rennie in *The End of the Road*. Summations of and influences on *The Sot-Weed Factor* and *Giles Goat-Boy* are included in an extensive way in the final novella.

Barth even reveals, within the context of "Bellerophoniad," that he set aside the mammoth project that was to become *LETTERS*, to complete the trilogy that became *Chimera*. Siphoning off bits of the novel-to-be, he incorporates Jerome Bray and Bray's work with computer-generated literature in "Bellerophoniad."

The last of the novellas in *Chimera* has been read by some critics, notably Harris, as being the most pessimistic of the three.[9] The argument advanced is that because Bellerophon rails against the way he is being put into print at the end of "Bellerophoniad" and because he is cut off in his and the novella's final remarks, his is the least satisfying of the resolutions in *Chimera*. Such a position ignores the excess Barth champions here and elsewhere. Of course, Bellerophon is unhappy. He would rather live and, failing that, gain classical stature by being mythologized. However, retelling his story without the digressions, corruptions, and embellishments Barth provides would have produced the kind of sanitized fiction *Chimera* is not. Each segment of *Chimera* dwarfs the one preceding it, just as each reshaping of a story must include the interpretations that went before it.

Notes

1. Jerry H. Bryant, "The Novel Looks at Itself—Again," *The Nation* 215 (18 Dec. 1972): 631.

2. Heide Ziegler, *John Barth* (London: Methuen, 1987) 60.

3. Charles B. Harris, *Passionate Virtuosity: The Fiction of John Barth* (Urbana: University of Illinois Press, 1983) 129.

4. David Morrell, *John Barth: An Introduction* (University Park: Pennsylvania State University Press, 1976) 142; and E. P. Walkiewicz, *John Barth* (Boston: Twayne Publishers, 1986) 111.

5. John Barth and Joe David Bellamy, "Having It Both Ways: A Conversation Between John Barth and Joe David Bellamy," *New American Review* 15 (1972): 145.

6. John Barth, *Chimera*, (New York: Random House, 1972) 8.

Further references will be noted parenthetically in the text.
  7. Morrell 162; and Harris 136.
  8. Harris 138.
  9. Harris 155.

CHAPTER EIGHT

LETTERS

Before and after its publication in 1979, *LETTERS* seems to have caused Barth more anguish than his other fictions. Asked by an interviewer about the length of time it took to write the novel, Barth exploded that it took all of his forties: "Let's say seven years, since the story runs to sevens, and it's my seventh book. Long enough to conceive a child and see it into grade school."[1] Barth interrupted *LETTERS* to write *Chimera*, which accounts for some of the difficulty in producing *LETTERS*. Its hostile reception by critics led Barth to be somewhat protective of the novel, calling it terrific in the interview published as "Speaking of *LETTERS*" in *The Friday Book.*

To the reader attracted to characters and incidents from Barth's earlier fiction and to the letter-writing format, which is used exclusively throughout the novel, *LETTERS* can be terrific. As in *Giles Goat-Boy*, the university is a central locale; it is, however, treated in a much less allegorical way in *LETTERS*. As in *The Sot-Weed Factor*, history is recycled; *LETTERS*, though, has a far more dazzling array of events recounted (most prominently, the War of 1812 and many occurrences from the 1960s). To the reader drawn to *Giles Goat-Boy* and *The Sot-Weed Factor* for the leisurely pace with which stories are often told, *LETTERS* might come as a shock; details, historical and invented, are offered at a dizzying rate.

LETTERS is an account of the "capital A Author" exchanging letters with some of his previous characters or their descendants as well as with a new character, Lady Amherst. Aside from "the Author" and Lady Amherst, the letter writers include Ambrose Mensch (*Lost in the Funhouse*), Jerome Bonaparte Bray (*Chimera*), Todd Andrews (*The Floating Opera*), Jacob Horner (*The End of the Road*), and A. B. Cook (a descendant of the Cookes and Burlingames of *The Sot-Weed Factor*). This book, like *The Sot-Weed Factor*, has as its literary antecedent an eighteenth-century model, in this case the epistolary novel as practiced by Samuel Richardson in *Clarissa*. Again, though, the use of such a form is not a neutral one; Barth opts for an established convention to bring out its stylized qualities as well as to engage contemporary topics. In his case, the play on the multiple meanings of letters—as missives, actual correspondence sent to people, and as the building blocks out of which words are composed—is accentuated, giving the updated letters of *LETTERS* that particular postmodern slant in which language is put in the foreground and realistic fiction is rejected. Unrelentingly, this is accomplished. Even the title draws attention to the letters in the word L E T T E R S.

LETTERS

Those seven letters are themselves composed on the title page of letters, in this instance, the ones that make up the novel's subtitle: "An old time epistolary novel by seven fictitious drolls & dreamers each of which imagines himself factual."[2]

To complicate and enrich further the status of letters, each of the letters sent by the various characters which constitute the chapters of the seven sections (marked by the letters L E T T E R S) is itself marked by one of the letters of the subtitle mentioned above. As if this were not enough, many of the letters that are written and sent in *LETTERS* are structured alphabetically instead of narratively. This ploy, used to emphasize that it is life which is parasitical to language, is featured in, for example, the wedding toast "The Author" delivers to Germaine Pitt and Ambrose Mensch:

Alle
Blessynges
Content that Cheereth ye
Darkest Days No
Enemy but many
Friend
Good Luck . . ." (770)

Mensch's last letter is also structured via the alphabet, and even the rhythm of his courtship of Germaine is dictated by the alphabet. Ambrose discovers that the following are the first four-syllable words (which, with some poetic license, are extended to five syllables) for each letter of the alphabet in his dictionary: "Ad-mi-ra-ti-on, Be-ne-fi-ci-al, Con-so-la-ti-on, De-clara-ti-on, Ex-hor-ta-tion, For-ni-ca-ti-on, Ge-ne-ra-ti-on; followed by Ha-bi-ta-ti-on, In-vi-ta-ti-on, & cet" (765). These are, in fact, the stages Ambrose and Germaine go through, the invitation referring to their wedding and the et cetera to their life afterwards.

Already, from these initial remarks, it should be apparent that this is the most demanding of all Barth's novels. Long and convoluted, it has a dazzling and encyclopedic array of allusions—drawn from politics, culture, and history, not to mention all Barth's fiction written before this one. Any novel that mentions contemporary novelists such as Doris Lessing, Iris Murdoch, William Styron, and John Updike, sixties' guru Timothy Leary, German writer Hermann Hesse, such people (living and dead) as Marlon Brando, Dante, Henry IV, Casanova, Hans Christian Andersen, Carmen Basilio (the boxer), Rosa Luxemburg, Sacco and Vanzetti—not to mention hundreds more—and provides abundant references to events in the sixties (the Mary Jo Kopechne incident, multifarious happenings in the Vietnam War, Supreme Court rulings, resignations and appointments—again to choose arbitrarily from a cascade of details), as well as activities surrounding the War of 1812, promises to provide a daunting read. The novel can be seen as an engagement with the status of language and letters; as a scrupulous examination of the sixties sensibility,

LETTERS

complete with copious amounts of drug-taking, sit-ins and other forms of student radicalism, and communal farms; or as a recapitulation of Barth's scope and focus in his earlier novels. *LETTERS* also includes a good deal of self-reflexive theorizing about the direction Barth is taking in the novel at hand.

Despite the many literary and historical allusions, the plot line of *LETTERS* is fairly straightforward. It proceeds rather mechanically, in fact, since plot is not particularly important to Barth in this work. Each of the seven (or rather eight as Cook IV gives way to Cook VI in chapter 4) letter writers in the novel writes, in the same order in the seven chapters, from one to five letters detailing his or her preoccupations. "The Author" gets the last word and his is one of the major levels on which *LETTERS* takes places. "Mr. John Barth, Esq., Author," as Barth calls him, relates self-consciously how he is producing the novel known as *LETTERS*, as well as its focuses and difficulties.

Lady Amherst, the one writer who does not appear in any of Barth's earlier works, corresponds exclusively with "the Author," relating her growing love affair with Ambrose Mensch and her British perspective on American culture. She operates on two levels, assessing Barth's previous output, thus relating to him as an equal, and interacting with one of his characters from *Lost in the Funhouse.*

Todd Andrews upsets the events that took place in *The Floating Opera* by updating the lives of the Macks and his increasingly complex involvement with them. Such a practice undoes the sense of finality that one usually gains from the end of a novel.

Jacob Horner continues to be the self-obsessed, confused figure he was in *The End of the Road*, writing most of his letters to himself. He, too, augments, but clouds, the stories of those with whom he was involved in the earlier work. The welter of allusions to historical figures is largely his contribution as he weaves names and dates into his otherwise claustrophobic self-scrutiny.

The confusion over progeny, parents, and lineage that was Barth's focus in *The Sot-Weed Factor* is now the obsession of A. B. Cook IV, as he documents the origins of Cooks, Burlingames, and Castines. Cook IV gives way to Cook VI to complicate further the story line as well as the blood line. As a descendant of Cook IV, Cook VI brings the Author, his progeny, and readers up to date, sketching American and personal history from the War of 1812 up to the novel's present.

Jerome Bray, the Satanic figure of *Giles Goat-Boy*, provides in *LETTERS* modes of communication antithetical to those of the humanistic, print-oriented Author. His computerized novel and plans for other high tech media cover most of the material the Author surveys in *LETTERS* via less mechanistic means.

Ambrose Mensch is no longer the sexually uninitiated teenager he was in *Lost in the Funhouse*. Indeed, by the end of *LETTERS*, he has been enmeshed in a torrid relationship with Lady Amherst; his letters in the final chapter announce their marriage.

The letter writers of *LETTERS* are complexly linked to the Author, his past fiction, and less fully, one another. Nonetheless, there is enough interaction among them in diverse ways to make their appearance in the novel an other than arbitrary one. While a reader of *LETTERS* who has not previously read other novels by Barth may be bewildered by the stories the major figures weave, he or she can also respond to their histories as those of any character with a richly detailed past who is introduced in a novel.

Unlike reviewers, literary critics who have studied *LETTERS* in the decade since its publication have found it to be rich with ideas and energy. Heide Ziegler sees this book and *Sabbatical* as twins, sharing a common origin in modernism and, strangely enough, marking Barth's return to realism.[3] This assessment was made before the publication of *The Tidewater Tales*, which is more certainly *Sabbatical*'s twin. Charles B. Harris, too, sees this book as a return from Barth's experimentation with avant-garde fragmentary stories to more substantial treatments of character and theme. He relates the fragmentary pieces to Barth's attitudes about the literature of exhaustion, but sees the later pieces as the affirmative synthesis implicit in the literature of replenishment.[4] E. P. Walkiewicz sees in *LETTERS* Barth's continuing concern with the role of the reader in the teller-tale-told complex.[5] This book is so fancifully and richly embroidered, however, that these observations only touch a few of the possibilities.

The most self-conscious of all of Barth's novels, *LETTERS* involves "the Author" often interpolating, explaining why he is doing what he is doing. At one point he argues for the benefit of "The Reader," "Currently I find myself involved in a longish epistolary novel, of which I know so far only that it will be regressively traditional in manner; that it will *not* be obscure, difficult, or dense in the Modernist fashion" (341). Uncapitalized readers are, no doubt, bemused by this comment. Although the novel contains only letters, the content of those letters and the relationships of those writing and reading them make this novel as dense a read as any this side of *Finnegans Wake*. Barth is, remember, an old-fashioned storyteller, except "now" that role can only be exercised ironically. He reintroduces stories about earlier characters of his not to augment those tales, but rather to call into question the conclusions that could be drawn from those happenings. Even more radically, this further deployment of previous players calls into question the autonomy of the work of art.

In postmodernism "work" or "book" gives way to the notion of text with no small shift in perspective. If book conjures up notions of completeness, unity, and organicism, text has no affinities with such purity. If the modern novel emphasized purity of construction, real structures, however complex, that are much more polished than the world outside the book, the postmodern novel, as it is extolled by Barth, is "that most happily contaminated literary genre: . . . *the Novel, with its great, galumphing grace, amazing as a whale!*" (151). There is nothing refined or dandyish about this kind of novel in general or *LETTERS* in particular; it is excessive and digressive.

"The Author" confides in Todd Andrews that "given your obvious literary sophistication, you will agree with me that a Pirandelloish or Gide-like debate between Author and Characters were as regressive, at least quaint, at this hour of the world as naive literary realism: a Middle-Modernist affectation as dated now as Bauhaus design" (191). *LETTERS* is no mere extension of the debate developed by, among others, Luigi Pirandello in a work such as *Six Characters in Search of an Author* and André Gide in *The Counterfeiters;* both those writers abandon realism and question the premises that allow authors to invent characters. Barth in *LETTERS*, though he does precisely that which he is making fun of, is pronouncedly postmodern in his use of the device for comic purposes, in this case to draw attention to the obsessive self-consciousness of twentieth-century art. Lady Amherst knows what Barth is up to. She chides, "the Author's" self-scrutinizing practices by writing, "To us Britishers, this sort of programme is awfully theoretical, what? Too French by half, and at the same time veddy American" (438).

As "the Author" asserts in one of his letters to "the

Reader," every letter exists in two different time frames, in its writing and in its reading, even when the post office does its job expeditiously; there is the possibility that very little of what prevailed when the writer wrote will still do so when the reader reads. To quote from the novel, "Despite March 2, 1969 being the date on the letter quoted in *LETTERS*, the letter was actually composed on October 30, 1973" (44). The novel's date of publication is 1979, whereas the events of the novel occur in 1969 (with numerous flashbacks to the nineteenth century). Despite all the data about the sixties mentioned by many of the letter writers in *LETTERS*, Barth late in the novel lets readers know that by "now" the Vietnam War has ended and Watergate is the current focus of attention in the United States. Even as that letter ends, its composition has moved the date "now" to January 1974 with its own newsworthy occurrences. Barth's desire to write "now"—which is an impossibility because, of course, once "now" is written, now is already then—returns in the last letter of *LETTERS*. Addressed again to "the Reader," its subtitle is: "*LETTERS* is 'now' ended. Envoir" (771). While the play with the word "now" might seem like trifling or philosophical nitpicking, it is important to the justification for Barth's rewriting of his own earlier works. Barth's "Author" can write without duplicating because, with time having passed and identities having shifted, the framework for the reception of material from previous books has been altered. To emphasize such fluctuations Barth provides three different dates for three different paragraphs in the last letter of *LETTERS*. To conclude this gambit Barth, in the final paragraph, offers the following: "You read this on [*supply date and news item*]" (772). Instead of offering pattern, order, or completeness at the end of this extended novel, Barth encourages readers themselves to continue the catalogue of dates, events, and writers.

Other focuses of Barth in *LETTERS*, some of which are similar to his concerns in *The Sot-Weed Factor* and *Giles Goat-Boy*, are as follows: the question of interpretation, that of identity, the state of academe, the sixties sensibility, and the relationship of film and literature. As was discussed vis-á-vis the other novels, attaching a meaning to the protean Barth is not only a difficult exercise, but it is also a wrongheaded one. About, for instance, the marshes, which played such an important role as setting in *The Sot-Weed Factor*, Barth, again self-consciously, provides in *LETTERS* a whole range of meanings for them: "Marshes: associated with both decay and fertility, female genitalia (cf. Freudians on Medusa), death and rebirth, miasma (pestilence, ague, rheumatism, sinusitis), evil, damnation, stagnation (e.g. Styx, Avernus; also Ezekiel 47:11). Behemoth sleeps in cover of reeds (Job 40:11), Marsh ibis sacred to Thoth, inventor of writing" (48). And on (in an extended way, always) goes this encyclopedic investigation of marshes in history and myth, augmented by allusions to Alexander the Great, Maryland, Irish bog-peat, and twelfth-century Chinese stories. What readers get here is the kind of disquisition usually presented by a literary critic seeking to explain the uses of marshes (their symbolic, mythic, metaphorical dimensions) in *The Sot-Weed Factor*. Such a preemptive interpretation, in a fictive context, serves to do two things: (1) problematize that venture in a critical work; (2) undercut the definitive meaning of something such as "marshes" in a literary text.

As to the question of identities, Barth's play with and destabilization of such characters as Harold Bray and Henry Burlingame, among others, reaches exaggerated proportions in *LETTERS*. The mysterious André Castine gets a genealogical profile that overwhelms any solid identity leaving him more ambiguously conceived and unfixed than Bray was in *Giles Goat-Boy* and Burlingame in *The Sot-Weed Factor*. The Bea Golden of *LETTERS* is given a more protracted "full" name at one point: Jeannine Patterson Mack Singer Bernstein Golden; she is later given the added title, Regina de Moninatrix, for her role with Jerome Bray and his computer, Lilyvac II. To unwind her name (itself perhaps a joke in the divorce-oriented contemporary era) would demand an epic tale that would not fix her identity because it would ignore her relationship with Reggie Prinz, the film director who frequently appears in the letters of various of the novel's writers. In an earlier novel, say *Wuthering Heights*, a genealogical chart would help identify the various Earnshaws and Lintons who people that novel; the two charts that are actually printed in *LETTERS* are meant to parody the importance and certainty of parents, lineage, and roots. Marsha Blank Mensch, another multiply-named character, adds the further surname, Horner, to her own by now impressive list, the three surnames linking her to *The End of the Road* and *Lost in the Funhouse*, as well as *LETTERS*. Probably more than any other postmodern writer, Barth swells his characters with meanings and attributes, moving them further and further away from the possibility of being interpreted as unitary, whole, and realistic.

Despite being an "old time epistolary novel" with postmodern concerns, *LETTERS* examines the sixties decade at length and with wit—though a bit testily. There is a sense in *LETTERS* that the campus disruptions of that era, while being sympathized with politically, are objects of satire because of the often sophomoric quality of those disruptions and the naive theoretical underpinnings that (barely) sustained them. It is rare that readers of his fiction can discern such unmediated anger, or if anger is too strong a word, disdain, on Barth's part. Lady Amherst, writing to "The Author," states that her secretary, Shirley Stickles, "cannot understand (I cannot always either) why the students who seize and 'trash' Columbia, extort ransom for the stolen paintings from the University of Illinois, force the resignation of the Presidents of Brown and CCNY, commit armed robberies at Cornell, and more or less threaten MSUC, are not even expelled and sent posthaste to Vietnam, far less put to the torture as she recommends" (206).

It appears that Barth, always with a subversive's sentiments, wants to check what was perceived to be a prominent tendency of that disruptive era; however, in more recent novels such as *Sabbatical* and *The Tidewater Tales*, written in a more conservative era, Barth wishes to confront a dominant drift that resides, this time, in the government. Nonetheless, in *LETTERS* student revolutionaries come off badly, in this case with Merope Bernstein and Drew Mack in unflattering revolutionary roles. Barth's wit is turned on the trendiness of figures such as "Goatee," who has been transformed into a terrorist by his reading of history at a black branch campus of the state university, and "Tank-Top" who was a child of affluent parents and "had discovered his negritude as a twelfth-former at the Phillips Exeter Academy" and "become a militant at Magdalene College (Oxford)" (95). Barth also teases hippies and their stylized attributes when he has Lady Amherst, who is after all the Acting Provost and Distinguished Visiting Professor at Marshyhope State University College, wear miniskirts, forgo brassieres, smoke marijuana, take LSD, and dance to bands such as The Who, Jefferson Airplane, and Pink Floyd. Quite clearly, Barth cannot commit himself and his pen to any cause or style; his sense of irony threatens to, and finally does, undo any fad, program or agenda. Barth is, in one sense, the least political of postmodern writers because he takes up no cause virulently or wholeheartedly, but also he is very political in his criticism of those elements that threaten the rights of both individuals and communities.

Despite the gibes at the rebelliousness and student life of the sixties, Barth is not vindictive about a group and milieu he observed at close quarters; nonetheless, there are some wonderful tongue-in-cheek comments about universities throughout *LETTERS*. While *Giles Goat-Boy* uses the university as a metaphor for the universe, it contains little about university practices and habits. *LETTERS* gives Barth an arena within which he portrays, among other things, the pettiness and intensity of academic politics. The initial letter of the novel, in fact, is written by Lady Amherst to "John Barth," offering him an honorary degree from MSUC, whose address is Redman's Neck, Maryland, a not very subtle allusion to the lack of a rich academic environment at MSUC. Here, Barth comments wryly on the decade of the sixties in which universities were spawned and/or grew with astonishing speed in places seemingly hostile to a scholarly sensibility. Lady Amherst mentions that MSUC has only recently emerged as a university, its predecessor being Tidewater Technical College—obviously a less esteemed institution of higher learning. Throughout the novel Lady Amherst is the primary vehicle for a comic assessment of the life on such a campus (which includes the jockeying for power by means of that honorary degree as well as other battles that, at one point, cost Lady Amherst and Ambrose Mensch their positions at the school).

Sometimes Barth's witticisms are sophomoric, his forte not being social commentary; however, his exploration of the world of letters—which introduces a third sense of the word, one that Barth does recognize and play on—is immensely sophisticated. Regarding this other aspect of letters, that of literature and culture, Barth has "the Author" write to Ambrose, introducing it along with the other two connotations of the word:

"Here's what I know about the book so far. Its working title is *LETTERS*. It will consist of letters . . . between several correspondents, . . . and preoccupy itself with, among other things, the role of epistles—real letters forged and doctored letters—in the history of History. It will also be concerned with, and of course constituted of, alphabetical letters: the atoms of which the written universe is made. Finally, to a small extent the book is addressed to the phenomenon of literature itself, the third main sense of our word Letters: Literature, which a certain film nut is quoted as calling that moderately interesting historical phenomenon, of no present importance" (654).

Impinging here is Barth's over-riding love of letters as literature (and literature as letters) and its current threatened usurpation by film, a seemingly more accessible medium that seemingly requires a minimum amount of literacy. Referred to in "the Author's" letter is Prinz's ubiquity, his incessant appearances in the novel, staging and framing events for the ever-devouring camera.

LETTERS

The film-literature debate assumes importance in this novel because, at the time of the writing of *LETTERS*, it had begun to assume cultural importance. The emphasis given the visual medium is, to a print-oriented and print-revering writer and thinker such as Barth, another target for his strategies of undoing. What with the popularity of films and the growth and sophistication of film studies at universities, the threat, rendered here comically, of course, is that "the Author" comes to be perceived as a presence as dated as Lady Amherst in her bell-bottom trousers. One of the scenarios in *LETTERS* is the proposed filming of one of Barth's books, a highly unlikely occurrence for his convoluted, metafictive works. Author subordinated to director is a motif Barth works with as Prinz energetically stages all kinds of theatrics so that he can, so he thinks, absorb reality with his camera, which appears to be an instrument able to capture and to present immediately the world "out there." The pen, or typewriter, by comparison works in a more delayed and more unwieldy manner. This is not to say that Barth disapproves of cinema per se; in fact, he has Ambrose mention in one of his early letters to "the Author" that James Joyce was tremendously interested in film. What Barth objects to is the privileging of another medium.

The premise of *LETTERS* is that the novel will never be supplanted by film—or by any technical achievement. In order to emphasize the value of letters generated by writers, throughout *LETTERS* Barth satirizes the attempt of Jerome Bray to program his computer to produce a book composed of numbers that will render letters superfluous with their ambiguity and complexity. Bray tells Bea Golden that currently popular media will be superseded by "coaxial television and laser holography, ultimately by a medium far more revolutionary, its essence the very key to and measure of the universe" (637). Such exaggerated notions about the progress and perfectibility of humans and their tools is antithetical to the language-based activities of Barth whose notion is that letters are as diverse and immutable as humans are, that people will always be "scratching out" their existence, however sophisticated the machines are that help them do it.

Notes

1. Barth, *The Friday Book: Essays and Other Nonfiction* (New York: Putnam, 1984) 177.
2. Barth, *LETTERS* (New York: Putnam, 1979). Further references will be noted parenthetically in the text.
3. Heide Ziegler, *John Barth* (London: Methuen, 1987) 64, 67.
4. Charles B. Harris, *Passionate Virtuosity: The Fiction of John Barth* (Urbana: University of Illinois Press, 1983) 160–61.
5. E. P. Walkiewicz, *John Barth* (Boston: Twayne, 1986) 128.

CHAPTER NINE

Sabbatical: A Romance

After finishing the "supra-realistic" *LETTERS*,[1] which resurrected many of his characters dating from *The Floating Opera*, Barth turned to a project close to his tidewater heart—sea stories. The first of these, *Sabbatical: A Romance*, published in 1982, affirms Barth's lineage within the American literary tradition of the romance, both as a form developing out of nineteenth-century American Romanticism and as romantic love. The book is not only about literature—though it is surely that—but about socio-political reality in America and the personal lives of a few close members of two families, the Turners and the Secklers.

In the early days of Barth's career, he indicated that he had no interest in contemporary social issues: "Muse spare me (at the desk, I mean) from Social-Historical Responsibility, and in the last analysis from every other kind, except Artistic."[2] In general, he adheres to this premise, for all his books self-consciously reflect on narrative art, but *Sabbatical* and *The Tidewater Tales* are also overtly political, moving from "the desk" into the mar-

ketplace of American ideology. They question, in Pyn-
chonesque fashion, the nature and extent of American
military-industrial links as well as the rapid wasting and
polluting of the natural environment. Admittedly, the
moral imperative is secondary to questions of storytelling
and narration, but it is there.

Of special concern, too, is the mutual love of *Sabbatical*'s two narrators, Fenwick Scott Key Turner and
Susan Allan Seckler, his wife of seven years. Arriving
back from a sabbatical spent sailing the Carribean, Fenn
and Susan plan how to resume their careers and family
responsibilities. In disgrace with the Central Intelligence
Agency for publishing *KUDOVE*, his exposé of their
activities, Fenn plans to write another book, and Susan
hopes to take up a teaching position at Swarthmore.
Upon their return they are confronted with the skull-
duggeries of CIA and Federal politics and the grim reminders of American drugs and violence as they have
affected Susan's sister, who had been on drugs and was
the victim of a multiple rape. But all is not negative:
Fenn and Susan muse over literature and writing strategies, speak of their love for each other, and discuss the
rich complexity of their extended families—Susan's
mother (Carmen) and her current boyfriend (Dumitru);
Susan's twin sister (Mim) and Mim's son (Edgar Allan
Ho); Fenn's twin brother (Count), who has probably
been executed by the CIA; Count's son (Mundungus),
who has gone to Chile in support of Allende and has
probably been killed; Fenn's own son (Oroonoko), who

considers his father childish and irresponsible; and Fenn's parents, who are good, honest, tidewater folk. This is a book about decision making in life and art as well as devotion to others.

Two recent books entitled *John Barth*, one by E. P. Walkiewicz (1986) and another by Heide Ziegler (1987), spend some time on *Sabbatical*. Walkiewicz finds this book more conventional than those immediately preceding it. He identifies its power as coming not from communication theory or metafictive techniques, but from quest romances with their fertility patterns, conventional water images, wish-fulfillment dreams, and rituals.[3] Ziegler finds the book more imaginative and asserts that this postmodern parody calls "the distinction between art and life into question."[4] Gordon Slethaug picks up on the sea imagery in the book, discusses the nature, purpose, and range of floating signifiers, and claims that the basic structure is one of elaborate play on the various significations of "floating."[5] Although the book is playful, it also affirms the power of the sea to restore the characters' spirits and creative energies.

Central to this book is the question of decision making in the face of ambiguity and ambivalent meaning. Neither Fenn nor Susan has an easy time making decisions: Their loss of the sailing chart leaves them vulnerable to storms in the bay; the loss of traditional American social guidelines concerning political behavior as well as abortion leaves them to agonize over their own moral responsibility; and their departure from conventions of nineteenth-century realism leaves the fiction they write awash in the tide of postmodernism. Life and art are both subject to change and variability. While the "felt ultimacies" do not depend upon the nihilism of Barth's earlier works, the characters must still figure their way in the real and metaphorical troubled waters of their milieu. In coping with "dilemmas, choices, channel-forks,"[6] they must uneasily make decisions about life and art, decisions that are both tributes to and departures from previous literary and social conventions.

A book that presents itself as effortlessly literary, *Sabbatical: A Romance* makes reference in several places to works and writers that have influenced it or, since it is a sailing narrative, served as markers and tacking points. These include the Egyptian papyrus of the shipwrecked sailor, Homer, Virgil, and the Arabian Nights, as well as Defoe, Melville, Twain, Stephen Crane, Conrad, and Poe. One of the two protagonists in *Sabbatical*, Fenwick Turner, compares himself at various times to these figures and their creations, for he finds that literary models are to be followed to discover the art of living and the art of reading and writing. According to Fenn, "at sea, in all but roughest weather, we read a lot: indeed, like any proper sabbatical, our long cruise has been among other things an immersion, beneficial but not nettle-free, in the sea of print" (231). Reading is not the only literary pleasure, and the delight in telling stories is compared to making love. Peter Sagamore, the

protagonist of *The Tidewater Tales*, expresses this sentiment and says it even better than Fenn:

We enjoy swapping stories . . . as much as swapping
kisses from head to foot and around the world by both
the equatorial and the transpolar routes.
  Sex and stories, stories and sex. Teller and listener
changing positions and coming together till they're unani-
mous.[7]

  The stories to which Barth most often refers are *The
Odyssey*, *The Thousand and One Nights*, *Don Quixote*, *Moby-
Dick*, *The Narrative of Arthur Gordon Pym of Nantucket*,
and *Huckleberry Finn*. Of these, *The Narrative of Arthur
Gordon Pym of Nantucket* serves as the main literary refer-
ent. Barth also shows an awareness of modern and
postmodern literature as well as poststructuralist theory:

Fenwick has now a clearer idea than he did last fall of
what's happened in the world of occidental fiction since
circa 1960, when he ceased to pay close attention to it:
the Beat Generation has degenerated, the Existentialists
no longer exist, the French New Novelists have grown
old, the Angry Young Men are middle-aged and petu-
lant, the Black Humorists are serious and tenured, the
Jews are assimilated, the Latinos are lively and expatri-
ated, the blacks and redskins pale by comparison, the
homosexuals are still clearing their throats, the new femi-

nists aren't impressive though numerous women writers are, Master Nabokov is dead, Master Beckett is silent, Master Borges has turned into Rudyard Kipling, . . . there's something called Postmodernism, . . . [and] literary-critical structuralists, deconstructionists, semioticists, and neo-Nietzscheans of Paris, New Haven, and Milwaukee. (231)

Such a context is worked, by Barth, into the seajourney tradition, allowing him to provide comments on writing while the sea journey continues. This combination sets up the most fundamental pattern and structure of ideas in the books: the relation of predictable oppositions and expected conclusions to indeterminacy—or, as in all of his earlier works, how patterning is frustrated.

In alluding to Edgar Allan Poe's work, *The Narrative of Arthur Gordon Pym of Nantucket*, Fenn explains to Susan that binarity or (with a pun implicitly in Poe's narrative) polar opposition characterized the nineteenth century: "Lots of people believed that at each of the earth's poles there was a great abyss. These twin abysses continuously swallowed up the ocean and continuously disgorged it somewhere along the Equator, maybe at the sources of the Amazon and the Nile, just as matter swallowed up in a Black Hole might reappear from a White Hole somewhere else in the universe" (363). The scientific thought that undergirded nineteenth-century cosmology and geography was dualistic and binary and embraced such typical oppositions raised in Fenn's statement as north/south, black/white, warm/cold, and land/sea.

Barth demonstrates his awareness of the binary principle through such comments on Poe, but he raises the issue in other ways as well. He writes of Fenn's observation on binary stars, thus reminding the reader of *Chimera*, an earlier incarnation of binarity: "Up over Susan's head Fenwick sees Perseus and Company; he looks for Algol, the eclipsing binary that in most renderings of the constellation is Medusa's winking eye" (317). In a related sense, Barth plays throughout on the word "double." Fenn refers to double agents, double cross, and says to one man, "Oh, well, then. I was going to say, you're got a dandy cover now for doubling, if you were of a mind to double" (147).

Within *Sabbatical*, the characters are themselves binarily drawn. Susan and Mim Seckler are twins, as are Fenwick and Manfred (Count) Turner, and Susan aborts her twins, Drew and Lexie, with the "double shlup from the vacuum aspirator" (332). Each a twin, Susan and Fenn together become double narrators of the book. To carry this binarity to the point of ingenuity, Barth characterizes Susan as a university professor whose primary study has been on twins, doubles, and schizophrenia in America literature. She is a "professional reader" of fiction and Fenn an "author"—author and reader creating yet another set of doubles. Sister-sister, brother-brother, author-reader, male-female, husband-wife—the binary double continues ad infinitum.

UNDERSTANDING JOHN BARTH

Double patterning also occurs. Although Fenn is the main narrator, he and Susan share narrative responsibility, and the narration changes from Susan/first-person singular to Fenn/first-person singular, and occasionally to Fenn-Susan/first-person plural. This handling of the narrative integrates both female and male perspectives, and its rhythm is especially interesting, since the style is not interrupted by quotation marks for attribution, and yet the two speakers are given equal time and value:

I get to see my new man's competence, if not grace, under pressure. His patience, reasonableness, and high flapping-point. His knowledgeability and range of experience, compared to mine. His knack for making almost anything work. His unaffectedness and general amiability. His good humor and spaciousness of heart. Plus, frequently, his penis.

I get to see my new woman's logistical good sense; her cheerfulness in adverse circumstances; her culinary resourcefulness and skill; the way she learns things fast and doesn't forget them; her enjoyment of all kinds of people and situations, and her canny assessment of them; her general pluckiness—I'd even say courage. Her spaciousness of heart. The number and variety of her passions. And lots of her skin. (196)

The parallelism demonstrated here is like that of other digressions and special scenes within the book which are equally shared by Fenn and Susan. For example,

SABBATICAL: A ROMANCE

Fenn speaks of his ordeal in Baltimore, meeting Dugald Taylor; Susan tells of her ordeal, entertaining Mim's unruly children. Later Susan shares her special trauma and Fenn his—her abortion and his heart attack.

Themes, too, are presented in *Sabbatical* as binary and are referred to as twins. After Susan aborts her twins, the two narrators decide to preserve their immortality through their writing: "this story, our story, it's our house and our child" (356–357). But writing is only one "child"; doing and loving is another, and the two become twins. As Fenn announces, both writing and loving "come first! How could either come before the other, except as one twin happens to get delivered earlier? The doing and the telling, our writing and our loving—they're twins. That's our story" (365). Twinship is less a matter of biological doubling than of perceiving and incorporating differences in order to expand, and not foreclose, human activities and attitudes.

The most frequent of the literary references in the book are to Poe and his works, and the allusions to Poe himself are operatively binary, since they occur within the context of allusions to Francis Scott Key, one concerned with narrative, the other song. Susan claims to be spiritually, if not physically, a descendant of Poe, and her middle name is Allan. She thinks of herself and Poe as nineteenth-century romantics, "Nervous. Unstable. Frenetic" (214). Fenn, on the contrary, claims his ancestry from Key, is named Fenwick Scott Key Turner, and thinks of himself and Key as eighteenth-century

men, "enlightened, rational, cool, optimistic, unecsta-
tic, self-controlled" (216). In addition, the boat that the
two sail on their sabbatical is called the *Pokey*, a nomen-
clature that they view as comprising their combined an-
cestral traditions—Poe-Key. Moreover, in the first part
of the narrative, as Susan and Fenn return from the
Caribbean, they are forced into a sheltered bay by a
storm; the island they call Key, and the harbor they call
Poe. These playful allusions draw attention to the preva-
lence of binarity.

The structure of *Sabbatical* demonstrates a similar
binarity with the narratives continually moving between
two (or more) points, like a ship tacking in the wind.
There is a sense of an ongoing process of setting out and
returning (Fenn's surname is, after all, "turner"), much
like Susan's description of a Vietnamese poetic form,
the luc-bat: "Our voyage might be compared to a luc-
bat: we have sailed back to our starting-place and on a
bit farther, from where we may or may not proceed"
(270). While Fenn and Susan are sailing up the Chesapeake, they recount the history of their meeting and
mating. The sailing narrative is thus contrapuntally interwoven with a history of their romance. These are
handled through a flashback or "fleshbeck," as they say:
"There's Poplar Island ahead. We'll have to flesh faster,
the way the years have fleshed since then." They then
add, "That week afloat was a perfect week. Idyllic
weather. Warm water to swim in at night, naked with
the noctilucae. Getting to know each other in those days

of sailing and talking. Eating each other up" (195). Only a little later, the couple "plot their course" for the future: whether both wish to have children, whether Susan wants to take up a position at Swarthmore, and whether Fenn will resume teaching and writing. Choices for narration and life are uttered together, so that the binary oppositions are seen as synthetic and integrative, not analytical and separate.

Not only do these narrative patterns suggest the importance of the binary oppositions, but the sense of genre does as well. As Walkiewicz observes, the book has a base in quest romances, but it is more than that: it combines mystery and fact, romance and realism, sailing and fiction, life and literature in order to create what Fenn calls the "Literally Marvelous" or "Truly Irreal" fiction (135). The binary relation of mystery and reality is handled in many ways. The presence of "Uncharted islands in familiar waters" (135) is one of the mysterious, marvelous, and fantastic issues that opposes realism in *Sabbatical*. Fenn's ever-returning *boina* (hat) is another, for he loses it and it always returns to mark a major turning point in his life. His inadvertent meeting with Dugald Taylor is, by his own reckoning, a 1,023,000-to-1 coincidence, and his ex-wife and present wife both separately citing Kafka within the same day may even be more coincidental. The appearance of Chessie the sea monster is equally amazing, and more on the order of the fantastic. Even the CIA activities assume an aura of mysteriousness: it is not clear whether Paisley is dead, or, if he is, whether he has committed suicide or been murdered; although Fenn's brother Count and nephew Mundungus have disappeared, it is unknown whether they are dead, or, if they are, whether they have been murdered; and it is not clear what has happened to the Soviet defector, Shadrin. Just as mysterious, even "magical," is the way both Susan and Fenn simultaneously dream that Count and Mundungus are dead; Carmen claims not only to have had visions of them but to have talked to the ghost of Count. Carmen herself believes in telepathy, extrasensory perception, and meaningful dreams—"visions, voices, apparitions, cards" (255). Susan and Fenn also both simultaneously have flashforward dreams that concern Fenn's death, the demise of stable relationships, the destruction of important places in Maryland, and even the collapse of the environment and the Western world—the "Last Shlup." The presence of such a "Mysterious Agency" (148) suffuses this romance, as does the "reality of the irreality" (135) and the irreality of reality. Finding realism a bore, Fenn juxtaposes and intersperses the supernatural, coincidental, improbable, and intuitive with the natural, probable, and rational. Says he: "The literally marvelous is what we want, with a healthy dose of realism to keep it ballasted" (136). And further, "Realism is your keel and ballast of your effing Ship of Story, and a good plot is your mast and sails. But magic is your wind, Suse. Your literally marvelous is your mother-effing wind" (137). These different generic strains may be binary and oppositional in nature, but it is their combination that drives the narrative onward.

Many of these binary combinations suggest a paradoxical reconciliation of opposites—a position that Fenn tries to affirm. He thinks of the *Pokey* as a "union of contraries prevailingly harmonious indeed but sometimes tense" (217). When he seeks alternatives, he argues for a paradoxical combination or confluence as one possibility: "Is a Y a fork or a confluence? Does the Chesapeake Channel diverge into York River Entrance Channel and York Spit Channel, or do they converge into the Chesapeake Channel? The one inbound, the other outbound; or, in tidewater, the one on floods, the other on ebbs. Analysis versus synthesis; 'male' versus 'female.' Sperm swim up; ova float down" (137). He conceives of ways in which alternatives can come together so that one does not necessarily preclude another: "He dreams our possible futures as a literal fork in the channel, or a series of such forks, each presenting us with the options of steering astarboard, aport, or astern" (319). A blending of opposites is also what Eastwood Ho envisions when he considers the implications of a Vietnamese luc-bat for the Seckler clan: "The 'male' and 'female' couplets are coupled like the couple: the poem is a loving, sportive sally between the 'truly wed,' such as Manfred and Carmen, so often apart, were; such as the singer wishes he and Miriam might be" (272). Carmen, too, hopes for a union of contraries and believes the fusion of sperm and egg to exemplify a union that is absolute, where the separate elements "become something both and neither" (241). Such a paradoxical affirmation, often suggested by the symbolic shape of the letter Y, sounds a great deal like Fenn's own paradox on sailing: "To go forward, we must go back" (244).

However desirable, a paradoxical union of opposites is not the conclusion of this romance. What Fenn and Susan remark of Poe's observations of the sky holds true for their book as well: "While from the perspective of Earth . . . our galaxy looks like the capital letter Y, 'in reality' it is a disc of stars, a flat swirl or Saturn-like ring" (235). The pattern of tacking observed earlier is significant in this respect. Fenn and Susan do not just sail from point a to point b, and from there home; the journey of the sailboat is endlessly deferred with no destination final. It pleases Fenn "to be headed neither upstream nor downstream, upwind nor downwind, but noncommittally across both breeze and tide" (332). It also pleases him that his floating narration can digress to include such details as the sighting of Chessie. Even the old adage that death is the conclusion of the journey is not entirely true in this book, for Fenn and Susan's journey is perpetuated and immortalized by their fiction. In a similar fashion, Paisley's, Count's, and Mundungus's lives are prolonged through the queries and narrative accounts of them. The book affirms the indeterminate and non-closed rather than the stability offered by paradoxical reconciliation.

This sense of indeterminacy relates to the lives of

the narrators themselves and their fiction. Although the loss of Fenn's boina marks major structural changes in his life—divorcing Marilyn Marsh, leaving the CIA, and writing his new book on loving and sailing, its loss and recovery is not predictable. Fenn and Susan learn to take life as it comes, make decisions that seem right to them at the time, and leave the rest to chance. Such a lesson is fully illustrated in the life of Havah Seckler: Having escaped from Communism and now surviving on a pacemaker, she is plagued by internal bleeding and arthritis, but, nonetheless, happily anticipates the future. She survives on chance, but chance itself is only provisional, and Fenn often feels at a loss to know who, what, or where he is. The night of his "fleshvorvert," he is not sure whether he is in "his and Count's bedroom at Key Farm? The bedroom of his and Marilyn Marsh's first apartment, in a student warren on St. Paul St. in Baltimore? His tourist-class stateroom on the *S.S. Nieuw Amsterdam* in 1960? A hospice for the indigently terminal?" (314). Consistent "selfhood" turns out not to be a significant issue, however, for he discovers that he can affirm pluralistic alternatives. Twinship as divided or narcissistic self gives way to the "image of our plural selves" and "our love for another" (332).

Binary opposition or paradoxical unity in narration also yields to indeterminacy. While the variations of first-person narration may generally predominate, Fenn and Susan consider a "unitized, shiftified, Cuisinarted" version of "first person as either observer or protagonist, and singular or plural, and reliable or unreliable. Third person objective, omniscient, or limited-omniscient so to speak. Third person limited-omniscient limited to protagonist or observer. Third person effaced" (232). They know the risks of such a combination but, at some point in the narrative, use them all. In a similar fashion, the form of *Sabbatical* includes dramatized portions, newspaper accounts from the *Baltimore Sun*, and American and Vietnamese poetry.

This "farmishing" of generic forms, the self-conscious consideration of them, and the discussion of their uses in other literary documents goes beyond paradox and is akin to the description of Count who, in his cloak-and-dagger days in the CIA, "was playing Marlon Brando playing Mister Kurtz in Francis Ford Coppola's film *Apocalypse Now*" (307). The proper sorting of genre and narrative roles and responsibilities becomes virtually impossible. Fenn himself is self-consciously aware of the implications when speaking of the tendency to regression in twins and especially when relating Susan's dream to Pym's journey:

From McHenry's ramparts, which are also *Pokey*'s cockpit, Susan sees the West sink into the sun, the sun into the galactic vortex like Odysseus's ship-timbers into Charybdis, or whatever-it-was into Poe's Maelstrom. *Pokey* himself is now become our galaxy, now our universe, rushing headlong into one of its own Black Holes like that legendary bird that flies in ever-diminishing circles until it vanishes into its own fundament; like Pym's canoe rushing into the chasm at the foot of the cataract at the southern Pole: a black hole aspirating, with a cosmic shlup, us, U.S., all. (321)

Fenn's belief that "the world's regressing like crazy" (285) is inherent in this view of infinite regress and entropy or decay.

Fiction represents a way for Fenn and Susan to acknowledge indeterminacy and regression, to embrace new possibilities, as well as to perceive and impose pattern upon the old. They do not need to conform to five-act theories of dreams, symphonies, or fiction, and the overall patterning does not need to conform precisely to the archetype of the wandering hero; details are left out and perhaps inserted in order to assist the overall pattern. As a case in point, when Fenn tells Susan of his encounter with Marilyn Marsh, he quotes her as saying, "Hold it till your sphincters rot" (310), but he then confesses that while she did not really say that, "that was the sentiment" (311). Moreover, he acknowledges that in order to fit events into a coordinated sequence, the fifth act of a dream, and presumably fiction, "allegedly reorchestrates elements of the preceding four into a grand finale" (323).

Since accounts of lives are artificially molded into patterns, Fenn maintains, "we ourselves may never know one another's whole story" (302); given this assertion, Marilyn Marsh's statement that Kafka's hunger artist is "the sole satisfied spectator of his own performance" (302) has a ring of truth. Lives are indeterminate and, despite literary patterning, will remain so. Consequently, Barth plays forcefully with indeterminate meaning and floating signification in the book. Edgar Allan Poe, for instance, is not just a counterpoint to Francis Scott Key, but with a minor shift in pronunciation, becomes Edgar Allan Ho, the illegitimate son of Eastwood Ho and Mim. Fenn's brother is variously called Manfred, Count, Fred, Manny, and the Prince of Darkness. This is a case of many signifiers and one signified. Floating signification, different meanings attached to the same sign or word, is nicely illustrated in Dumitru's and Carmen's view of earrings on men; one earring is a sign "of a passionate nature. Add a second earring, Carmen says, and you've got a problem. Add a red neckerchief and a little monkey, her friend replies with a shrug, you've got an organ grinder" (266). Since Count has married Susan's mother, he is Fenn's brother and stepfather, and Carmen becomes his mother-in-law and sister-in-law. The book thrives on such playful permutations of sound and sense.

The sense of indeterminacy and discontinuity occurs strongly in the issue of maps. When Fenn and Susan come back from their sailing sabbatical and enter the Chesapeake, they are in familiar waters that have been extensively charted. In fact, Barth even refers to the map of the Chesapeake published in the *National Geographic* magazine. These charts and their unassailable presentation of facts are available to everyone, but when

SABBATICAL: A ROMANCE

Fenn and Susan inadvertently lose their sailing chart 12221 in a storm, they are directed to an island that they do not recall and that does not appear on any of the maps they subsequently inspect:

> No Key.
> Incredulous, we ask the clerk, the manager, and later the marina operator and our neighboring yachtsfolk. No one knows of a Key Island in Chesapeake Bay. Someone reasonably supposes it might be the local name for one of the small islands in the Goodwin or Guinea cluster: but none shares just the right configuration, elevation, and water depth, not to mention the large breakwater with its flashing beacon, surely charted. (132)

This situation raises questions about the reliability of information. For the average person, charts and maps are incontestable, especially in an area of the world settled as long, traversed as much, and mapped as frequently as this one. To be mapless and chartless is discomfiting, but to have faith destroyed in existing charts and maps is wholly unnerving. Fenn doubts, however, whether "even the Agency, with its crazy budget and all its new toys, could build an uncharted island smack in the middle of Chesapeake Bay, with full-grown woods and natural coves and marshes, or disappear a natural island from all charts past and present without anyone's blowing the whistle" (312). Charts give assurance of the human ability to explore an area, map it, and return again with reasonable assurance that things will not have changed; they validate rational observation and predictability. But Barth's book denies the totally predictable and raises questions about the chartless, mysterious, and unpredictable.

The conclusion of Barth's book reinforces this notion of indeterminacy, for the conclusion disrupts the narration. Fenn and Susan hunker down in the cockpit while they decide to stop sailing and start writing; the termination of their journey marks a turn to narrative. This is a new tack, a fundamentally different and hitherto indeterminate direction, but nonetheless necessary and engaging.

Also disruptive of Barth's narrative is the relationship between text, notes, and prefaces. In realistic texts and informational documents, the text is given central primacy. Deemphasized, reduced in size and significance, footnotes usually offer support and additional information without detracting from the main thrust of the narrative; prefaces and afterwords are also deemphasized, introducing and summarizing, but rarely providing primary information and argument. Contrary to this usage, Barth, in his footnotes, provides background information on Fenn and Susan, their family, and their boat; this information includes names, ages, family connections, professions, and interests. Even the fact that the book itself has been constructed from Fenn's journal is first provided in a footnote. Specific documentation about the CIA, Chilean police activities, and Russian intelligence operations, upon which so many questions in the narrative hinge, is given in footnotes. But certain playful bits of information are also given, including the mortality rate for striped bass as compared to human sperm. Then, too, the footnotes contain such apparently peripheral matters as Fenn's poem to the stinging medusa jelly fish. These details nearly create a second or double text, but their main function is to provide real or reputed facts, while the text itself is charged with the function of interpretation. In this way Barth marginalizes what is usually considered central and centers what is often believed marginal. For him the most important function is the perception and understanding of facts, not the simple recording of them. In decentering his text, he decenters the reader's conventional understanding of texts.

In the process of driving the narrative onward, this indeterminacy also raises the fundamental question of trustworthiness—especially of information. The issue of uncharted Key Island is always perplexing to Fenn and Susan, but Fenn himself happens upon information to suggest that the CIA has deliberately kept the island's location and existence a secret. At Doog's funeral, he overhears that Marilyn Marsh will take a helicopter to BARATARIA at Key Island where women junior officer trainees "are taught all the skills of their male counterparts—martial arts, tradecraft, and the rest—plus the tactical use of sex" (305). This discovery suggests that the paucity of information on Key Island is deliberate disinformation. The communication act is sabotaged, so charts, maps, and newspaper accounts are just as fictional as fiction itself. Public information has been deliberately shaped and distorted in order to mislead readers.

Barth seems to assert that *all* use of language is distorting. How is the average person, or, particularly in Barth's case, the average reader to know what is factual and truthfully informative, as opposed to what is a calculated lie or even an uncalculated one? To what end, Barth seems to ask here, as he did in *Lost in the Funhouse* and *Chimera*, is the communication act offered? Fenn and Susan try to communicate with each other, but find that they, too, withhold information at certain times. The CIA presents so much information, much of it contradictory, that the observer cannot help being perplexed. The role of "information, disinformation, even super-disinformed supercoded disinformation" (113) helps to "explore the waters" of the communication act and the human condition. Such problematic communication suggests new and positive possibilities.

Sabbatical does not affirm the merely traditional; oppositions or the harmonious reconciliation of opposites give way to capricious, chaotic, even entropic, indeterminacy. Still, the book does affirm the human ability to survive, prosper, and become artistic in the face of personal anxiety and social discontinuity, but it does not, and cannot, resolve the complex questions of the gaps in human communication. This is not a despairing book;

it is ultimately a comic vision of the broad range of limitations, human dilemmas, and possibilities for mankind.

Notes

1. The term supra-realistic is used by Heide Ziegler, *John Barth* (London: Methuen, 1987) 64.

2. Quoted in *The Sense of the Sixties*, ed. Edward Quinn and Paul J. Dolan (New York: The Free Press, 1968) 440.

3. E. P. Walkiewicz, *John Barth* (Boston: Twayne, 1986) 141.

4. Ziegler 80.

5. Gordon E. Slethaug, "Floating Signifiers in John Barth's *Sabbatical*," *Modern Fiction Studies* 33 (Winter 1987): 647–55.

6. John Barth, *Sabbatical: A Romance* (New York: Putnam, 1982) 173. Further references will be noted parenthetically in the text.

7. John Barth, *The Tidewater Tales: A Novel* (New York: Putnam, 1987) 114.

CHAPTER TEN

The Tidewater Tales: A Novel

John Barth's latest fiction, *The Tidewater Tales: A Novel* (1987), is another sailing narrative, continuing a tradition that, in certain respects, goes back to his first work, *The Floating Opera*. But this book, along with *Sabbatical*, conveys a fluidity and openness that did not characterize earlier works in the canon. Taking place on Chesapeake Bay, the book recounts the sometimes sunny and sometimes tempestuous relationship of Peter and Katherine Sherritt Sagamore, the proud owners of the sailboat *Story*, lovers of storytelling, and mentors of Franklin Key Talbott who is introduced as the "true" author of *Sabbatical*.

As in *Sabbatical*, the story is told by twin narrator-protagonists (Peter and Katherine), who vacation on the waterways of Chesapeake Bay while waiting for Katherine to come to full term. Their time is spent with a variety of family members and friends, including Katherine's parents, Henry and Irma Sherritt, her brother Chip, and friends Franklin and Leah Talbott, who provide intelligent conversation on parenting, sailing, and

THE TIDEWATER TALES: A NOVEL

writing, in addition to opinions on issues of CIA involvement and global pollution. As Richard Lehan observes,
"their major preoccupations involve the sea, sex and
stories, and the tales we hear are mostly about seamen
and semen, navigation and narration, textuality and sexuality."[1] The book is about the possibility of, and need
for, creativity and productivity (in both raising a family
and writing) in the face of a seemingly desperate, bru-
tal, chaotic, and entropic world. Barth's world is filled
with evil characters and impediments to constructive
action, but narrative helps the characters hear about
those who have succeeded in the face of extreme despair. The book ends happily with Katherine Sherritt
delivering twins, Leah Talbott pregnant, and Peter Sagamore and Frank Talbott with enough background material to write their next works, *The Tidewater Tales* being
Peter's own production.

The narrative takes place during a fortnight of sailing (June 15 to June 29, 1980), but, as Barth makes clear
in the elaborate table of contents, a fortnight is not a
fortnight. By counting the first twenty-four hours as
Day 0 and then narrating events and stories daily through
Day 14, Barth has created "The Fortnight and One," a
modern parody of *The Thousand and One Nights*. Narration and time are consequently linked. Premodern ways
of perceiving reality, including time and art, are called
into question even as they were in this book's twin,
Sabbatical, which interrogated binary systematizing. *The
Tidewater Tales*, too, escapes the confines of the binary

structure and affirms indeterminacy, which is integrally tied to the issues of social responsibility and storytelling.

It is too early to assess the critical reception of *The Tidewater Tales,* but Barth's own comment about his books can be taken as the operative principle here: by his own admission, Barth's books come in pairs, and *Sabbatical* and *The Tidewater Tales* are twinned more than the others, to the extent that, in good part, they must be viewed together. Not only are both sailing narratives with recurrent characters, but *The Tidewater Tales* is about the actual process of Franklin Key Talbott's conceptualizing and drafting *Sabbatical. The Tidewater Tales* is a wonderful resource book on the process of selecting, ordering, and editing the experiences of a novel. In one of the many interchanges on this process, Frank tells Peter how he has changed the names of his family to meet the needs of his proposed book:

I turned Rick Talbott into "Manfred Turner," because Doug Townshend called him the Prince of Darkness after Byron's Count Manfred. Lee and I were "Fenwick Turner" and "Susan Seckler." He smiles at her. Black-eyed Susan, right? My idea of the art of fiction was to make her and "Mimi" twin sisters and Fenn and Manfred twin brothers. You're supposed to nudge your neighbor and say, "Fen as in marshland, et cetera." Carla B Silver became "Carmen B. Seckler," for reasons even I am too embarrassed to tell.[2]

THE TIDEWATER TALES: A NOVEL

Frank documents the way an author will change names and events to make art like, but separate from, life. He indicates that in certain situations such as that of John Arthur Paisley, the CIA agent who has disappeared, historical information can be taken wholly into fiction, without changes of attribution. He shows that some experiences are wholly imaginary. And he acknowledges that the job of thinking through and writing a work is rarely done single-handedly; others help the author with ideas, plot structure, and basic literary techniques. In this way, these two books by Barth are integrally combined, so that when one depends upon binary opposition and indeterminacy, the other will also depend upon that—though upon other things as well.

Perhaps the most obvious binary, oppositional relationship between the two is established in the subtitles of *Sabbatical* and *The Tidewater Tales* themselves; the first is described as a romance and the second as a novel. Although various definitions of these modes apply, within the romance problems are generally resolved, love is requited, and the structure is governed by marvelous occurrences and coincidences. The novel usually emphasizes realistic events, deals with the socio-psychological makeup of the main characters, documents the culture of a given period, and depends upon cause and effect. To some extent, these conventions do apply in the respective books. *Sabbatical* is about the relationship of Fenn and Susan, their maturing love for each other, and mutual decision to let their lives be extended through fiction rather than offspring. These decisions, as with previous major ones, are marked by the magic of the ever-returning boina, an event supplemented by the even more fantastic sighting of Chessie, the sea monster. *The Tidewater Tales*, conversely, deals with family life, especially of the heroine's, the circle of friends that gather to hear the telling of tales, as well as the major social and political issues currently affecting the lives of Americans. Obviously fantastic elements such as the sighting of Chessie are omitted, and the *boina*, which moves from storyteller to storyteller, becomes the badge of narration. The central mystery is Paisley's body floating into sight, and, so far as coincidences are concerned, the greatest is the similarity between the fictional account of May and June in a play called *SEX EDUCATION*, which Katherine fishes from a canister in the Bay, and the real story of May Jump and Katherine Sagamore. In the course of the story other coincidences occur to the extent that Peter apologizes for the "Too-Far-Fetched Coincidence" or "Implausible Possibility" (402). The book does, however, deviate from strict realism and include some amazing details, for what could be more fantastic than the appearance of Peter's double or of Odysseus, Nausicaa, Don Quixote, and Scheherazade? Probably the greatest difference between the two books is that, from the perspective of *The Tidewater Tales*, *Sabbatical* is fiction that has been written by Franklin Key Talbott. In that sense, *Sabbatical* is a romance and *The Tidewater Tales* a novel, the one imagined, the other a real procedure. But that distinction also breaks down, for Barth is, of course, the author of both books; the binary opposition is an extension of his creative imagination, and these books are literary fabrications that draw attention to their own fabricating.

The style of the two books is important and in certain respects can also be binarily compared. As one of Barth's shorter works, *Sabbatical* is more unified than *The Tidewater Tales:* its time is restricted to a few days, its place to a small portion of the Chesapeake, and its action to relatively few events in Susan's and Fenn's lives. As one of Barth's longer works, *The Tidewater Tales* sprawls: it takes place during a fortnight and a day in a fairly large area of the Chesapeake, and it goes back in time and space to ancient Greece and medieval Spain. About the only aspect of this book that is condensed is the ever-present acronyms, but those are only short forms for much broader titles and topics. The sprawling nature of this narrative is indicated by an internal subtitle: "The Tidewater Tales, or, Whither the Wind Listeth, or, Our Houses' Increase: A Novel" (83). The Houses' Increase not only consists of the twins that Katherine finally delivers and who are, among other things, binarily named Nice and Easy, Said and Done, Blam and Blooey, Tick and Tock, and so on, but also the superabundance of characters. In the penultimate episode, for instance, when the flotilla of sailboats, *Story, Reprise, Katydid IV,* and *Rocinante IV,* are anchored together, nearly all the crew tell and listen to stories. These include Peter and

Katherine Sagamore and their unborn twins; Katherine's parents, Henry and Irma Sherritt, and her brother Chip; Franklin and Leah Talbott, her mother Carla B Silver, her sister Marian, and her nephew Sy; and Marian's current lovers, May Jump and Donald Quicksoat. These fourteen characters, who correspond with the fourteenth day of the sail, are in the course of the book supplemented by scores of other characters.

The Tidewater Tales is an inexhaustible text, and, while the main issue may be one of indeterminacy, the abundance of narratives and characters provides a response to the issue of exhaustion. In his 1967 essay, "The Literature of Exhaustion," Barth announced that realistic fiction had run its course and was effectively dead to new possibilities. Although some critics assumed incorrectly that this essay was about the impossibility of writing, "The Literature of Replenishment" (1979) makes clear that if for the present-day person certain traditional forms and ways of looking at fiction (and reality) are exhausted, then other useful alternatives will emerge. In talking to Leah, Carla B Silver addresses this issue when she speaks of Leah's pregnancy—her increase or replenishment—in the face of environmental and political catastrophe: "The world is wrecked and poisoned, friends: just about done with. But you guys are right to go on with it, all the same. Look at the pair of you! Look at that afternoon out there! So you'll be A-one parents, and they'll be dynamite kids! That can hurt the world?" (361). Though Leah opts for fiction rather than children

THE TIDEWATER TALES: A NOVEL

as her "increase," the metaphor of exhaustion and replenishment is still meaningful in this novel of abundance and exuberance, one that clearly exceeds *Sabbatical* in its narrative inexhaustibility.

The two books also differ in style in another significant way. Whereas *Sabbatical* plays with the relationship between footnotes and text, *The Tidewater Tales* omits footnotes, but sets up a play between chapter, title, and story. The chapter titles occupy nine pages in the table of contents and range from the single-word exclamatory title, "Well!", to one that runs well over a page in length, significantly longer than the actual narrative for that chapter, which consists of only one word, "Ahem" (73). In two other cases the chapter titles are followed only by three-dot ellipses. These titles sometimes provide summaries of the content of the section, serve as the transition between two sections, act as the transitional comments of a character, or serve as the first words of a section. Both books are consistently playful and mark Barth's love of word play and formalistic ingenuity.

The books' double narrators, who are accorded more-or-less equal responsibility, also seem on the face of things to emphasize binary opposition, but go beyond that. While in *Sabbatical* the two narrators are Fenwick Key Turner and his wife, Susan Allan Seckler Turner, in *The Tidewater Tales* the "coupled point of view" (29) consists of Katherine Sagamore and her husband, Peter. A librarian, Kate is "39 years old and 8½ months pregnant," Peter "39 years and 8½ months old." The repetitive rhetoric of these descriptions underscores the couple's equality, for they are evenly matched opposites. Intelligent and beautiful, she was raised in upper-class, WASP Dorchester County; handsome and literate, he in lower-middle-class Hoopers Island. She is Rabelaisian, he Cartesian. She likes long sentences and he short: "If Less Is More is Pete, More Is More is Kath. Pete's pet poet is Emily Dickinson: *zero at the bone.* Katherine Sherritt's is Walt Whitman: *I contain multitudes*" (29). Each, in turn, is teller and listener, narrator and reader, for "a mouth needs an ear, an ear a mouth" (25).

On their boat, the two narrators entertain a host of other sailors and relatives, for *Story* is their narrating sailboat which they take on their "ad-lib" cruise, just as their BMW is their "Expository Vehicle." Primary among their visitors are their counterparts, Franklin Key Talbott and Leah Allan Silver Talbott. Talbott is the author of an exposé on the CIA called *KUBARK (KUDOVE* in *Sabbatical),* and Leah is a professor of American Literature who encourages his endeavors to write interesting narratives. As it turns out, the Talbotts are the "real" figures behind the narrative personae, Fenn and Susan. These pairs are, in turn, the narrative manifestations of John Barth (if not of other writers). This duplication within duplicitous duplication exceeds the boundaries of binary opposition, and the narrative disappears within itself, an example of infinite recursiveness. Barth describes such a situation in the course of the Homeric tale about Penelope weaving her lovely tapestry:

THE TIDEWATER TALES: A NOVEL

Even the casual viewer noticed and properly admired the little panel-within-a-panel, but there was a further detail known only to the maker and one other. In an area no larger than her fingernail (in a tapestry itself wall-size), she had managed to suggest in the tiniest stitches of the very finest thread the scenes from Panel One, being woven in Panel Two, being woven in Panel Three. That idea she had gotten from Phemius, who, as he sang of Troy, once improvised an interlude wherein an old minstrel entertains disguised Odysseus with a song of the war itself, in course of which is described the shield forged for Achilles by the gods, on which in turn is figured the story of the war thus far. (195)

Sabbatical is, then, the nucleus of a clever and innovative frame tale, which is revealed and supplemented by numerous other small framing devices in *The Tidewater Tales*. An ancient device, dating back at least to Giovanni Boccaccio, and one that Barth has himself examined in "Tales Within Tales Within Tales," an article that appeared in *Antaeus* and later was included in *The Friday Book*, the frame device is usually restricted to a single book, but Barth has considerably expanded the technique. He first experimented with this device in *Lost in the Funhouse*, where "Menelaiad" concerns the art of storytelling. There Barth designates the frame device through quotation marks within quotation marks, tales within tales. *Lost in the Funhouse* itself depends upon something of a frame device, for Ambrose Mensch in *LETTERS* confirms his authorship of *Lost in the Funhouse*.

Since he was a central character in *Lost in the Funhouse* and an aspiring author, the revelation of his authorship comes as no real surprise. However, to find that Talbott is the real author of the Susan-Fenn narration is truly surprising and, accordingly, more original. To have a single book that is the central frame of a frame tale revealed in the second book is highly innovative and delightfully handled. By this device, Barth plays with binary opposition, considerably extends the limits of the frame device, and centers both books on the development of a literary imagination.

Closely related to this frame device and binary opposition is Barth's playful mixing of texts. The blurring of distinctions between *The Tidewater Tales* and *Sabbatical* is one instance, and another is the self-conscious, intertextual relationship between the play *SEX EDUCATION* and the story "Night-Sea Journey" of *Lost in the Funhouse*. Whereas "Night-Sea Journey" is told from the point of view of the sperm or swimmers, the play is told from the point of view of the ova or floaters. These accounts of the sperm and ova, as Katherine herself points out, recall *The Odyssey* and the wanderings, final homecoming, and values of the hero. Certain portions of *SEX EDUCATION* also recall *Sabbatical*, especially June's and the Swimmer's quandary at the confluence about whether to go upstream, downstream, or remain where they are. The intertextual parallels do not end there: June's floating downstream is reminiscent of Peter's setting out on the river at the age of thirteen and

THE TIDEWATER TALES: A NOVEL

Huck Finn's childhood journey. In fact, when Peter charts his excursions, he realizes that he links the literary and the local: "Huckleberry Findley on the Honga River; Odysseus Dmitrikakis on the Little Choptank; Captain Donald Quicksoat outside Fawcett's Marine Supply store in Annapolis Harbor . . ." (472). Rather than a frame tale, this is a looping device known as the Moebius, where one pattern follows nearly identical chartings, but always with a difference. These recurrent patterns are not strictly alike or oppositional; they are improbably coincidental, and deal with the infinite and partially unpredictable permutations of cultural and literary forms. This, too, is a kind of indeterminacy.

Double narration and authorial responsibility in *The Tidewater Tales* is unpredictable and decentered in yet another way, for the process of storytelling is not the exact and simple matter of an author writing a book or of one or two narrators telling a portion. Peter is not the author, or at any rate the sole author, of his fiction. He does manage to tell of his own childhood experiences, but Katherine tells of her own. Similarly, Frank and Leah both tell of their experiences and concerns as does Leah's mother, Carla B Silver. Katherine's former lover, May Jump, also narrates a portion. These are the contemporary figures. Among others who tell their tales are Odysseus and Nausicaa (Theodoros and Diana Dmitrikakis), Don Quixote (Captain Quicksoat), and Scheherazade. It is Douglas Townshend who suggests that the rogue agent, Frederick Mansfield Talbott, is re-

ally the Faust of the CIA and should be called Manfred—
characterization that is picked up in *Sabbatical*. In addition, these figures talk and criticize the works they have
read. Chip, Katherine's brother, offers interpretive comments on James Joyce's "Araby"; Peter on *Huckleberry
Finn* and some works of Freud and Jung; and Katherine
on the three-act drama, *SEX EDUCATION*. In effect,
this book suggests that stories are not divinely intuited
by one author, but are the carefully constructed product
of current and historical linguistic, literary, and cultural
experiences. Writing and narrating become collective concerns that involve scores of people, both contemporary
and ancient.

When Peter tried to be the sole author, he stag-
nated and was unable to move from his minimalist philosophical position that "Less is More." He consequently
risked losing his readership: "Though nowise obscure
or difficult, Peter's art is without pizzazz, and ever terser.
The cognoscenti cheer; the larger public, regrettably,
ignores him, and, regretfully, he them" (25). His fiction
had been reduced to little more than a title. By listening
to others during those fourteen and one days of sailing
on the Chesapeake, he accumulates sufficient experiences and tales to create a massive book that proclaims,
"More is More." He reverses his position and adopts
Katherine's.

Despite the contributions of others to the narrative,
it is still the responsibility of the main storyteller or
author to link them together and fashion them. Whether

the stories concern the interchange of tales by Odysseus and Nausicaa, a fortnight of sailing on the Chesapeake, or the sex education of May and June, someone such as Phemius, Peter Sagamore, or Frank Talbott must put them together. It is that task especially that so enrages Odysseus, because he fears that Phemius will put his "private offense into public art, multiplying the felony" (192). The artist's role, perhaps even his duty, is to take the personal and the public and make it universal. Consequently, Barth often makes his most poignant character the minstrel or writer. Phemius, whose eyes are put out by Odysseus, has not had an easy life but is able to take common materials and construe them beautifully and universally. The artistic genius is "not a person dramatically different from ordinary people. He is a man or woman much like others, but more finely honed, to the point where his difference in degree becomes almost a difference in kind." He or she is one who can sing "with a discernment, an economy, a pungency of detail, and an artfulness of arrangement" (200).

As important to this concept of authorial talent is the reader's interest and perceptiveness. On several occasions in his fiction Barth addresses the importance of the readers in assuring the immortality of art, and calls them "the Mother and Father of Invention" (410). The story of Scheherazade and Dunyazade told by May suggests that, as in *Chimera* earlier, the role of the reader in creating the fiction equals the author's:

Well, it didn't take sharp Dunyazade long to realize that if their visitor was truly from the future, where there existed a book with a happy ending about herself and Shah Zaman and Scheherazade and Shahryar, then et cetera and *voila*. The genie not only told Scher what to do—which is to say, he reported to her that what she had done in the story was tell the king stories—but told her as well which stories she told, and in what order, and where to interrupt them to best dramatic effect. (584)

Author and reader reflect each other just as *The Tidewater Tales* and *Sabbatical* do.

The use of multiple storytellers and of authors and readers is only one of several reflecting devices within the book. This book (as with *Sabbatical*) begins and ends with similar poems and double thunderstorms, measured in Peter's terms as "Blam! Blooey!" which bracket the "story like artillery zeroing in" (23). They also provide a clue that the beginning of the story is much the same as the ending: the end of sailing and listening to stories marks the beginning of writing them. This paradox, first fully articulated in *Lost in the Funhouse*, is emphasized by the concluding punctuation using a colon rather than a period and by the presence of the title page at the opening and conclusion of the tale. At the end of the narrative Peter compares Katherine's unfinished poem to Penelope's incomplete tapestry and Scheherazade's unfinished tales; these, in turn, help iden-

THE TIDEWATER TALES: A NOVEL

tify the open-endedness of the book. That *The Tidewater Tales* extends the narration of *Sabbatical* fully demonstrates that the process of narrating and writing is an unending one.

Additionally, the books, like the stories within, have no final destination; they are concerned with process, not product. True, in *Sabbatical* the couple is homeward bound from their Caribbean sabbatical, but they discover that the end is not what they had in mind, that it is rather a beginning. *The Tidewater Tales* is even more playful, a voyage of the Sagamores "without itinerary timetable or destination," a fortnight of "sailing whither the wind listeth . . . [with] certain small or large adventures and maybe telling each other stories as they [go] along, some they've never told before and some they know by heart but need or want to hear again or tell the kiddies; some real stories from their life together and their lives apart; some made-up stories; some found stories and some lost stories" (76). Katherine refuses final goals and asserts that "destinations are just excuses for sailing." Just as a sailing boat is not designed to go directly and quickly from destination to destination, so these are stories with a leisurely pace and no center or ultimate purpose. The stories themselves provide the momentum to drive the sailboat forward: "our twin narratives had fetched us wing and wing through the warming forenoon . . ." (127). This is what they call "narrative navigation" (209). They are stories which are designed to be told slowly, with little purpose other than the

telling of them. They are, in one of the primary metaphors of the book, "the new clothes" which "have no
emperor" (85). Or in terms of the Sherritt family seat,
Nopoint Point, they are stories whose long term goal is
to have no final goal.

While both books emphasize sailing itself and depend upon the metaphor of sailing, their content is nicely
balanced between socio-political events and the art of
storytelling. Katherine and Peter are equally devoted to
politics, as were Fenn and Susan, so both books inter-
mingle political concerns with sailing and literature. In
Sabbatical the book concerns the CIA, especially as em-
bodied by John Arthur Paisley, Manfred "Count" Turner
and his son Mundungus, and Dugald (Doog) Taylor. In
The Tidewater Tales, the CIA activities include the life
and death of John Arthur Paisley, as well as those figures in *Sabbatical* who appear with new nomenclatures:
Frederick Mansfield Talbott and his son Jonathan, and
Doug Townshend. Their deaths are closely tied to the
government's manipulation of the media and interfer-
ence in the lives of key political figures as well as ordinary citizens. Even more horrendous is the CIA's clandestine manipulation of governments in Chile, Cuba,
and Iran. Peter claims, on his behalf and Katherine's,

What we're against, sentimental stock liberals that
we are, is our government's collusion in—not to say its
systematic, well-funded direction of—assassination, torture, clandestine warfare, the clandestine undermining

THE TIDEWATER TALES: A NOVEL

of other people's elected governments, the clandestine harassment of and illegal general snooping upon our own citizens—things like that, you know, by anybody from our intelligence community down to our local cops. (238)

To this list they add "nuclear proliferation, the U.S. economy rusting out, the natural environment clogging up, the national infrastructure crumbling away and no money to rebuild it" (66). Because Katherine feels so incensed about the foolhardiness of the U.S. involvement in foreign governments, she helps form a society called HOSCA—"Hands Off South and Central America."

Although not so obviously universal in scale or cosmic in consequences as government intervention, local prejudices lead to global intolerance and intervention. Peter recognizes that people acquire these like they do a disease, almost unconsciously, but certainly. Like Mark Twain, he must write his way through his own prejudices in order to exorcise them; whether prejudicial attitudes grow out of his boyhood environment or are acquired elsewhere, he needs to think and write about them to loosen their hold.

As destructive of collective rights and individual freedom is the deliberate pollution of the environment, a concern that is not raised in *Sabbatical*. This issue is close to both Katherine and Peter, for his father's farm has been used by a New Jersey firm for industrial discharges and toxic waste, and Katherine discovers that her brother Willy and ex-husband Poonie are both involved in illegal disposal of waste. These are the people—businessmen and politicians—who are polluting the Chesapeake and Potomac beyond repair. They are the indecent folk, well heeled and well bred, who ought to know better, but who, because of greed, are killing the planet.

Equally problematic is the irresponsible behavior and disease associated with America's postsixties sexual permissiveness. *Sabbatical* documents the horrifying rape of Mim Seckler at the hands of a motorcycle gang and a redneck pervert, and *The Tidewater Tales* treats that and other aspects of America's quickly changing sexual practices in a pre-AIDS society. Katherine tells of her adolescence, which, despite Poonie Baldwin's insertion of the forest green crayon in her rectum, was relatively innocent. Even her postmarital affairs with Yussuf al-Din, Saul Fish, and Jaime Aiquina have an air of innocence about them, for they are relationships of deep love and, at least in one case, political conscience. Her relationship with Poonie was less innocent, for, before their marriage, he gave her crab lice, and during their marriage, in a drunken rage, he raped and tortured her, not understanding or acknowledging the origins and manifestation of his homosexuality. His sordid sexual practices following the failed marriage are not as explicitly detailed as those of Katherine's brother Willy, who abandons his wife sexually and engages in one-night stands with "brass-and-fern pickups," ultimately contracting "the social disease of our American times, herpes simplex"

THE TIDEWATER TALES: A NOVEL

(52). This he conveys to his wife in their rare coupling, and she, "after this story's close," dies of cervical cancer. Freedom from Victorian restraint in sexuality does, then, create a mixed response. For Peter and Katherine, it means they can make love before marriage without feeling guilty, that they can strip and go swimming naked with Chip, that they can enjoy a healthy hedonism: "Chip offered to swim the other way, but no, no: We embraced him, too, and despite our nudity he allowed our hug. This isn't sex, Andrew; it's the being here together at last—where we'd no more than half-seriously wished the wind would fetch us—full of stories and babies and the knowledge that our time is all but upon us" (523). For others who lack their responsibility, sexuality can be damaging. Such a message extends the implications of Mim's rape depicted in *Sabbatical*; the sexual revolution, as Peter muses, can create joyful opportunities but does require responsibility: "The beauty of women, Donald Barthelme somewhere proposes, makes of adultery a painful duty. Thinks Peter, standing hands on hips, Yes, well: And love makes of fidelity a manageable responsibility" (424).

Because the United States has so abused its power, and its citizens, their individual freedoms, the narrators in both books like to think of alternatives that are not only pleasant but necessary. Storytelling and writing are the preferred ones and provide a way of coping with catastrophic events. *Pokey*, the sailboat in *Sabbatical*, is transformed to *Story* in *The Tidewater Tales*, and Katherine is the founder of ASPS—the American Society for the Preservation of Story-telling—which suggests her devotion to literature. To some, storytelling will seem a refusal to reckon with the larger social and political issues; for them storytellers are either blindly unaware of their ultimate fate or bravely refusing to be overwhelmed by the tragedy, death, and destruction that surround them. The storytellers in this novel are, however, not blind to any consequences, but believe that language itself is a way to cope with reality, for as Scheherazade maintains, "language is a more amazing thing than flying carpets and crystal palaces" (588). Her literary and sexual encounters with Djean (Peter), who goes on "Metaphorical Excursions" to visit her, fully articulate the notion that language is capable of bringing people together from different PTOR—"place and time and order of reality" (590). Rather than perpetuating prejudices and creating problems, language can magically bridge and heal.

The use of language in the novel creates art, and art can affect life. Odysseus finds that life imitates art when Nausicaa sits on Phemius's manuscript and acquires freckles similar to Penelope's. Odysseus and Nausicaa especially discover the power of metaphor when they "whistle up a breeze" and "sing up a storm" to provide the wind for their journey. When they together sing the unending frame-tale from *Lost in the Funhouse*, "There was a story that began once upon a time there was a story that began . . ." (224), their boat flies beyond the limits of space and time. Scheherazade, too, finds that when she repeats the magic formula, WYDIWYD (What you've done is what you'll do [594]) or TKTTTITT (The key to the treasure is the treasure), she can alter space and time. These expressions both suggest that language determines our reality, and that language is not bound by all the conventions of time and space. Peter's graduate-school girlfriend, Jean Heartstone, espoused a "Magic Language Theory" (309), which, stripped of the rhetoric of magic, signifies that language does create reality. If language is the main tool of cognition, then whatever we write helps to express our culture. It is both our way of creating and dealing with reality. Telling stories does help solve problems.

Consequently, Barth is both serious and playful when comparing aspects of writing to the workings of the CIA, the American political process in transition from Carter to Reagan, the pollution of the environment, and the changing sexual mores of Americans. There is a certain fluidity and movement to all of these, for a relationship does exist between changes in political integrity and the loosening of novelistic techniques. But Barth does not allow himself to be caught in the trap of irresponsible relativity. The United States' destruction of legitimate governments in other countries is absolutely wrong, while a breakdown in novelistic techniques may be quite fine. In the first instance, the United States has no business deliberately undermining the stability of other governments, whereas for a writer anything is game, for writing is a game, though a game that reveals reality.

The Tidewater Tales is a complex book that can be favorably compared to *Sabbatical* but which can stand by itself. In its pursuit of the indeterminate as well as social and literary analysis, it presents the readers with a rich and extended reading experience.

Notes

1. Richard Lehan, review of "The Tidewater Tales: A Novel" in *Los Angeles Times Book Review* (June 28, 1987): 10.

2. John Barth, *The Tidewater Tales: A Novel* (New York: Putnam, 1987) 413–14. Further references will be noted parenthetically in the text.

CHAPTER ELEVEN

Conclusion

The last word insofar as it is written about John Barth should notably be offered as "the last word," indicating that one should be skeptical of summations, fixities, overviews. This is so not merely because Barth is still alive and still earning a living as a writer, but also because any such attempt conflicts with the notion saturating Barth's fiction that writing is a continuous activity, one that results not from an artist's doctrinaire desire to say something, but from language's richness and Barth's love of redistributing it. As long as there are men and women writing, all texts can be regarded as pre-texts that engender other texts that, in turn, become further pretexts.

The last word on postmodern fiction has also, of course, not been written. Barth, who teaches a seminar in fiction writing at The Johns Hopkins University, can observe the impact of his own work on youthful writers. In a recent unpublished interview, Barth provided an incisive sense of directions that seem to be popular. While the experimental, self-conscious work that he,

UNDERSTANDING JOHN BARTH

Pynchon, and Coover, among others, have popularized remains an important literary model, there is another movement, what can be called the neorealist school, that has gained adherents recently. Probably because of the surfeit of innovative, highly elaborate works that find their sources in a novel such as *LETTERS* or *The Sot-Weed Factor*, the simpler, more transparent, flatter stories of Raymond Carver, Ann Beattie, and Richard Ford, which do not include references to the manipulating, language-absorbed novelist, have gained their own adherents and imitators. Delineating mundane or turbulent moments in the lives of middle- or lower-middle-class Americans, these works do not have the same intellectually relentless aspects of Barth's. Nonetheless, Barth, ever gracious and unobsessive, does not think that fiction necessarily needs, exclusively, the parodic, self-scrutinizing style that *Understanding John Barth* has sought to explain and, perhaps, champion.

No doubt there will be other rich, protracted playful works from Barth. Unlike Pynchon's extremely complex voice and Barthelme's terse, wry voice, Barth's is an effortless, chatty one which produces humor and density out of the many stories he loves to tell. Among all the writers of metafiction, it deserves repeating, Barth's engagement with fiction stems least from social, political, or theoretical urges; rather, the love of language and narrative, as well as the self-consciousness towards them, defines his reason for writing. Even the most cryptic passages of *Lost in the Funhouse* result from too many

CONCLUSION

stories instead of from derailing or denying one central story line. Bray, Burlingame, and Ambrose, among others, tell enough tales to fill even more volumes than the voluminous ones Barth has produced. As Heide Ziegler writes, "The capital A Author is the ultimate hero of Barth's fiction."[1]

For someone who gained notoriety with the dense, convoluted experiments with technique in *Lost in the Funhouse*, Barth is the least committed of all the postmodernists to transforming story continually into radical frames. One gets the sense that Barth, above all, could have flourished in any period, weaving tale upon tale to celebrate the act of fiction-making. That he was born into writing in the mid-to-late twentieth century prods him to write self-consciously about, but affectionately with, the means of storytelling that precede him by centuries. His up-to-date qualities get grafted onto tradition, constantly changing it. Many of the characters in Barth's canon (including the recycled "John Barth" of *LETTERS*) are authors, turning experiences into stories. The most captivating, indeed, are the ones who produce them most prolifically.

The most recent novels, *Sabbatical* and *The Tidewater Tales*, correct a tendency to embrace art exclusively at the cost of contemporary political realities. Instead of such composite figures—that is, figures constructed from myth and literature—as Giles Goat-Boy and Joan Toast, the major characters in the later novels are more realizable. Moreover, they engage in their own specific ways such topics as sexism and American imperialism. While still not as obsessed with confronting social constructs as is Coover, Barth does not ignore the contextual nature of the reality in which he currently lives. Again, in the interview mentioned above, Barth gave the following sense of his own political dynamic: In the upheaval of the 1960s, which Barth witnessed from his vantage point at various universities, it was not especially necessary to oppose authorities who were already beleaguered; in the neoconservative 1980s, however, opposition becomes more important as its practitioners become less numerous.

Nonetheless, it is not as a politically engaged writer that Barth will gain, or rather, has gained, his stature. Any attempt to read him simplistically or definitively will not only be fruitless, but it will also destroy the heart of his work, which is to say, the production of a multiplicity of signs, of letters, the reading of which will always be altered by time, by history, by idiosyncracies of readers and by continued rewriting of authors. Those who want stasis, fixity, solid answers might as well wait for Jerome Bray of *LETTERS* to develop his LILYVAC computer to the point where it produces a novel out of numbers, instead of slippery, evasive letters.

Understanding contemporary American literature and American culture would in many ways be facilitated by understanding John Barth's writing. An attraction to plenitude, to meanings spawning meanings, to

CONCLUSION

a surplus of value as demonstrated in his works is anti-thetical to a society that, though it appears to love financial and material excess, wants its political and theoretical currency kept simple. Barth is, in many ways, furthest from the fundamentalist temperament that grips part of the United States. The demand for bedrock meaning emanating from one incontrovertible source, the Bible, is something Barth resists. His fiction is a pluralist's delight, in its size, energy and abundance of story lines. No one statement is allowed to rest firmly as the source and center of all others.

At one point in *LETTERS* Lady Amherst sets herself the task of devouring and assimilating "John Barth's" life work. Writing of "the heft of your *oeuvre*," she promises to study the fiction, "never ceasing till I shall have overtaken as it were the present point of your pen" (4). Less daunting tasks exist in the annals of literary criticism. Only Barth's undercutting of his output, his own stance as author, saves sprawling works such as *LETTERS* from being ponderous, from calling too plainly to be considered great literature. A writer such as Norman Mailer, perhaps, writes long novels to invest himself as well as his text with stature. Despite the vast amount of erudition in his novels, Barth presents a much more disarming presence; he reveals no interest in writing "the great American novel," except parodically to reduce such a concept. Even amongst many postmodernists there is occasionally the sense that the craft of fiction and its effects on readers should be taken, despite the jokey nature of the texts, very seriously. Such a perspective, full as it is of self-aggrandizement, is full of illusions about fiction's place in American life.

Art is often thought of by critical commentators alarmed at America's supposedly vacuous culture as a panacea, some wonderful cure that will inspire people to read only classical literature, or works thought to be deserving such a title. Not for Barth this kind of hype. Indeed, through the course of *LETTERS*, among others, art in that genteel mold is itself mocked and derided. Canonizing the author via an honorary degree is made light of in that novel; it is seen to be a product of political maneuvering. Yet, again having it both ways, Barth reveals his love of literature, from anonymous limericks, to *Oedipus Rex*, to his own novels that get their critical evaluation in *LETTERS*. That that love, even of such august pieces as *Oedipus Rex*, is an irreverent one does not detract from the pleasure Barth derives from the texts he has absorbed. He is not a remote novelist, one whose deployment of scholarly elements removes him from contact with his readers; rather, the stories are connecting instead of estranging. A lover of stories and of storytelling, Barth also values readers, those who respond and seek to understand his own inventions and speculations.

CONCLUSION

Notes

1. Heide Ziegler, *John Barth* (London: Methuen, 1987) 86.

SELECTED BIBLIOGRAPHY

Works by John Barth
Books

The Floating Opera. New York: Appleton Century Crofts, 1956; rev. ed., Garden City, N.Y.: Doubleday, 1967; London: Secker & Warburg, 1968.

The End of the Road. Garden City, N.Y.: Doubleday, 1958; London: Secker & Warburg, 1962; rev. ed., Garden City, N.Y.: Doubleday, 1967.

The Sot-Weed Factor. Garden City, N.Y.: Doubleday 1960; London: Secker & Warburg, 1961; rev. ed., Garden City, N.Y.: Doubleday, 1967.

Giles Goat-Boy; or, The Revised New Syllabus. Garden City, N.Y.: Doubleday, 1966; London: Secker & Warburg, 1967.

Lost in the Funhouse: Fiction for Print, Tape, Live Voice. Garden City, N.Y.: Doubleday, 1968; London: Secker & Warburg, 1969; with "Seven Additional Author's Notes," New York: Bantam, 1969.

Chimera. New York: Random House, 1972; London: André Deutsch, 1974.

LETTERS. New York: Putnam, 1979; London: Secker & Warburg, 1980.

Sabbatical: A Romance. New York: Putnam, 1982; Harmondsworth: Penguin, 1983.

The Friday Book: Essays and Other Nonfiction. New York: Putnam, 1984.

The Tidewater Tales: A Novel. New York: Putnam, 1987; London: Methuen, 1988.

Uncollected Short Stories

"Lilith and the Lion." *Hopkins Review* 4 (1950): 49–53.

"The Remobilization of Jacob Horner." *Esquire* (July 1958): 55–59.

SELECTED BIBLIOGRAPHY

"Landscape: The Eastern Shore." *Kenyon Review* 22 (1960): 104–10.

"Test Borings." *Modern Occasions*. Ed. Philip Rahv. New York: Farrar, Straus, & Giroux, 1966. 247–63.

"Help! A Stereophonic Narrative for Authorial Voice." *Esquire* (Sept. 1969) 108–9.

Selected Uncollected Essays

"A Gift of Books." *Holiday* (Dec. 1966): 171–72, 174, 177.

"Censorship—1967: A Series of Symposia." *Arts in Society* 4 (1967): 265–358.

"A Tribute to Vladimir Nabokov." *TriQuarterly* 17 (Winter, 1970): 350. Also in *Nabokov: Criticism, Reminiscences, Translations and Tributes*, edited by Alfred Appel, Jr., and Charles Newman. Evanston, Ill.: Northwestern University Press, 1970.

"A Tribute to John Hawkes." *Harvard Advocate* (Oct. 1970): 11.

Preface to "Lost in the Funhouse." *Writer's Choice*, edited by Rust Hills. New York: David McKay, 1974.

"*Teacher:* The making of a good one." *Harpers* (Nov. 1986): 59–65.

"Postmodernism Revisited." *The Review of Contemporary Fiction* 8 (Fall 1988): 16–24.

Works about Barth

Interviews and Statements

Bellamy, Joe David. "Algebra and Fire: An Interview with John Barth." *Falcon* 4 (Spring 1972): 5–15.

———. "Having It Both Ways: a Conversation Between John Barth and Joe David Bellamy." *New American Review* 15 (April 1972): 134–50. Reprinted as "John Barth." *The New Fiction: Interviews with Innovative American Writers*, Urbana: University of Illinois Press, 1974. 1–18.

SELECTED BIBLIOGRAPHY

Cooper, Arthur. "An In-Depth Interview with John Barth." *Harrisburg Patriot* (30 Mar. 1965): 6.

David, Douglas M. "The End Is a Beginning for Barth's 'Funhouse.'"*National Observer* (26 Sept. 1968): 19.

Enck, John J. "John Barth: An Interview." In *The Contemporary Writer: Interviews with Sixteen Novelists and Poets*, edited by L. S. Dembo and Cyrena M. Podrom, 18–29. Madison: University of Wisconsin Press, 1972.

Gado, Frank, ed. "John Barth," in *First Person: Conversations on Writers and Writing*. Schenectady, N.Y.: Union College Press, 1973. 110–41.

"Hawkes and Barth Talk About Fiction." The *New York Times Book Review* (Apr. 1979): 7.

Henkle, Roger. "Symposium Highlights: Wrestling (American Style) with Proteus." *Novel* 3, no. 3 (1970): 197–207.

LeClair, Tom and Larry McCaffery, eds. "A Dialogue: John Barth and John Hawkes," in *Anything Can Happen: Interviews with Contemporary American Novelists*. Urbana: University of Illinois Press, 1983. 9–19.

Liebow, Cynthia. *"Entretien avec John Barth." Delta: Revue du Centre d'Études et de Recherche sur les Écrivains du sud aux États-Unis.* 21 (Oct. 1985): 1–15.

McKenzie, James. "Pole-Vaulting in Top Hats: A Public Conversation with John Barth, William Gass, and Ishmael Reed." *Modern Fiction Studies* 22, no. 2 (1976): 131–51.

Meras, Phyllis. "John Barth: A Truffle No Longer." *New York Times Book Review* (7 Aug. 1966): 22.

Prince, Alan. "An Interview with John Barth." *Prism* (Sir George Williams University) (Spring 1968): 42–62.

Reilly, Charlie. "An Interview with John Barth." *Contemporary Literature* 22, no. 1 (1981): 1–23.

SELECTED BIBLIOGRAPHY

Ziegler, Heide and Christopher Bigsby, eds. "John Barth," in *The Radical Imagination and the Liberal Tradition: Interviews with English and American Novelists*. London: Junction Books, 1982. 16–38.

Bibliographies

Vine, Richard Allan. *John Barth: An Annotated Bibliography*. Metuchen, N.J.: Scarecrow Press, 1977. Provides listings of primary works and extensive annotations on selected secondary sources.

Weixlmann, Joseph. *John Barth: A Descriptive Primary and Annotated Secondary Bibliography, Including a Descriptive Catalog of Manuscript Holdings in United States Libraries*. New York and London: Garland, 1976. An invaluable, comprehensive descriptive listing of primary and secondary works through 1974.

Books

Harris, Charles B. *Passionate Virtuosity: The Fiction of John Barth*. Urbana: University of Illinois Press, 1983. Primarily concerned with Barth's use of metafictive language techniques.

Joseph, Gerhard. *John Barth*. Minneapolis: University of Minnesota Press, 1970. Pamphlet; general introduction to Barth and his fiction.

Morrell, David. *John Barth: An Introduction*. University Park: Pennsylvania State University Press, 1976. A detailed account of the writing and publishing of Barth's works; an astute critical commentary.

Tharpe, Jac. *John Barth: The Comic Sublimity of Paradox*. Carbondale: Southern Illinois University Press, 1974. Places Barth's work within the context of dualism and synthesis.

Waldmeir, Joseph, ed. *Critical Essays on John Barth*. Boston: G. K. Hall, 1980. Previously published reviews and articles.

SELECTED BIBLIOGRAPHY

Walkiewicz, E. P. *John Barth*. Boston: Twayne, 1986. A general introduction to Barth's works, emphasizing their formal complexity, technical virtuosity, and wit.

Ziegler, Heide. *John Barth*. London: Methuen, 1987. Considers the playful, parodic quality of Barth's works.

Sections of Books

Allen, Mary. *The Necessary Blankness: Women in Major American Fiction of the Sixties*. Urbana: University of Illinois Press, 1976: 14–37. Barth's sympathetic depiction of women.

Caramello, Charles B. *Silverless Mirrors: Book, Self and Postmodern American Fiction*. Tallahassee: University Presses of Florida, 1983: 112–30. Barth's relation to current critical theory.

Fogel, Stanley. "The Ludic Temperament of John Barth," *The Postmodern University: Essays on the Deconstruction of the Humanities*. Toronto: ECW Press, 1988: 113–23. (Previously published in *Fantasy Newsletter*, July 1982.) The playfulness and irreverence of Barth.

Gorak, Jan. *God the Artist: Novelists in a Post-Realist Age*. Urbana: University of Illinois Press, 1987: 145–91. Explores Barth's comic invention of *topos*.

Hauck, Richard Boyd. *A Cheerful Nihilism: Confidence and "The Absurd" in American Humorous Fiction*. Bloomington: Indiana University Press, 1971: 201–36. Barth's absurdist tendencies—his use of parody and imitation.

Karl, Frederick R. *American Fictions 1940–1980: A Comprehensive History and Critical Evaluation*. New York: Harper & Row, 1983: 444–87. Treats the anti-authoritarian, anti-systematic impetus in Barth's works.

Klinkowitz, Jerome. *Literary Subversions: New American Fiction and the Practice of Criticism*. Carbondale: Southern Illinois

SELECTED BIBLIOGRAPHY

University Press, 1985: 3–17. Barth's postmodern narrative techniques in *Sabbatical*.

McConnell, Frank D. *Four Postwar American Novelists: Bellow, Mailer, Barth and Pynchon*. Chicago: University of Chicago Press, 1977: 108–58. Barth's concern for self-conscious and inauthentic fiction.

Safer, Elaine B. *The Contemporary American Comic Epic: The Novels of Barth, Pynchon, Gaddis, and Kesey*. Detroit: Wayne State University Press, 1988: 50–78. Barth as a Rabelaisian writer in *The Sot-Weed Factor* and *Giles Goat-Boy*.

Scholes, Robert. *The Fabulators*. New York: Oxford University Press, 1967: 135–73. An influential study, this book argues that *Giles Goat-Boy* is a modern fabulation or allegory.

———. *Fabulation and Metafiction*. Urbana and Chicago: University of Illinois Press, 1979: 75–102, 118–23. Treats *The Sot-Weed Factor*, *Giles Goat-Boy*, and *Lost in the Funhouse* as books about the process and order of writing—metafictive works.

Schultz, Max F. *Black Humor Fiction of the Sixties: A Pluralistic Definition of Man and His World*. Athens: Ohio University Press, 1973: 17–42. Discusses the absurd in *Lost in the Funhouse*.

Stark, John O. *The Literature of Exhaustion: Borges, Nabokov, and Barth*. Durham: Duke University Press, 1974: 118–75. A consideration of Barth's irrealistic techniques in relation to his own definition of "exhaustion."

Tanner, Tony. *City of Words: American Fiction 1950–1970*. London: Jonathan Cape, 1971: 230–59. Relates Barth's verbal play to Wittgenstein's work on logic and language.

Tilton, John W. *Cosmic Satire in the Contemporary Novel*. Lewisburg, Pa.: Bucknell University Press, 1977: 43–68. Focuses

SELECTED BIBLIOGRAPHY

on *Giles Goat-Boy* in relation to works by Kurt Vonnegut, Jr., and Anthony Burgess.

Critical Articles

Appel, Alfred, Jr. "The Art of Artifice." *The Nation* 207 (28 Oct. 1968): 441–42. The self-conscious, cerebral, witty, and parodic elements in *Lost in the Funhouse.*

Bell, Steven M. "Literature, Self-Consciousness and Writing: The Example of Barth's *Lost in the Funhouse.*" *International Fiction Review* 11 (Summer 1984): 84–89. Draws attention to writing as the subject of Barth's writing.

Bienstock, Beverly Gray. "Lingering on the Autognostic Verge: John Barth's *Lost in the Funhouse.*" *Modern Fiction Studies* 19 (1973): 69–78. Discusses the notion of identity in *Lost in the Funhouse.*

David, Jack. "The Trojan Horse at the End of the Road." *College Literature* 4 (1977–78): 159–64. Classical allusions in *The End of the Road.*

Edelstein, Marilyn. "The Function of Self-Consciousness in John Barth's *Chimera.*" *Studies in American Fiction* 12 (Spring 1984): 99–108. Emphasizes that readers must participate in shaping a work such as *Chimera.*

Farwell, Harold. "John Barth's Tenuous Affirmation: 'The Absurd, Unending Possibility of Love.'" *Georgia Review* 28 (1974): 290–306. Discusses the tenuous affirmation of love in *Lost in the Funhouse* and denies that Barth is nihilistic.

Graff, Gerald. "Under Our Belt and Off Our Back: Barth's *LETTERS* and Postmodern Fiction." *TriQuarterly* 52 (Fall 1981): 150–64. Reads *LETTERS* specifically and postmodernist fiction generally as claustrophobic.

Guzlowki, John Z. "No More Sea Changes: Hawkes, Pynchon, Gaddis, and Barth." *Critique* 23 (Winter 1981–82): 48–

SELECTED BIBLIOGRAPHY

59. Explores the view that these contemporary artists use sea imagery ironically to suggest the impossibility of psychological and spiritual renewal.

Hawkes, John. *"The Floating Opera* and *Second Skin." Mosaic* 8 (1974): 17–28. Links Hawkes' novel with Barth's, finding similarities in their works.

Hinden, Michael. *"Lost in the Funhouse:* Barth's Use of the Recent Past." *Twentieth Century Literature* 19 (1973): 107–18. *Lost in the Funhouse's* indebtedness to James Joyce and Modernism.

Kiernan, Robert F. "John Barth's Artist in the Funhouse." *Studies in Short Fiction* 10 (1973): 373–80. Explores the coherence of *Lost in the Funhouse.*

Knapp, Edgar H. "Found in the Barthhouse: Novelist as Savior." *Modern Fiction Studies* 14 (1969): 446–51. The mixture of myth, masque, cinema, and symposium in *Lost in the Funhouse.*

LeClair, Thomas. "John Barth's *The Floating Opera:* Death and the Craft of Fiction." *Texas Studies in Literature and Language* 14 (Winter 1973): 711–30. Self-invention as the key of this and other novels by Barth.

Malvern, Marjorie M. "The Parody of Medieval Saints' Lives in John Barth's *Giles Goat-Boy; or, The Revised Syllabus." Studies in Medievalism* 2 (Fall 1982): 59–76. An interesting yoking of the medieval and the postmodern.

McDonald, James L. "Barth's Syllabus: The Frame of *Giles Goat-Boy." Critique* 13 (1972): 5–10. Discusses the Posttape, Postscript, and Footnote in *Giles Goat-Boy.*

Mercer, Peter. "The Rhetoric of *Giles Goat-Boy." Novel* 4.2 (1971): 147–58. Observations on the hero.

Robinson Douglas. "Reader's Power, Writer's Power: Barth,

SELECTED BIBLIOGRAPHY

Bergonzi, Iser, and the Post-Modern Period Debate." *Criticism* 28 (Summer 1986): 307–22. Contemporary theories of reader response and postmodernism.

Rovit, Earl. "The Novel as Parody: John Barth." *Critique* 6 (1963): 77–85. States that as a parodic writer, Barth suffocates his fictions.

Schulz, Max F. "Barth, *LETTERS,* and the Great Tradition." *Genre* 14 (1981): 95–115. Examines the way Barth echoes Cervantes in fusing fact and fiction.

Slethaug, Gordon E. "Barth's Refutation of the Idea of Progress." *Critique* 13 (1972): 11–29. Barth's debunking of American positivism.

————. "Floating Signifiers in John Barth's *Sabbatical.*" *Modern Fiction Studies* 33 (1987): 647–55. Indeterminacy of form and content in *Sabbatical.*

Tatham, Campbell. "The Gilesian Monomyth: Some Remarks on the Structure of *Giles Goat-Boy.*" *Genre* 3 (1970): 364–75. The influence of Lord Raglan's *The Hero* on *Giles Goat-Boy.*

Woolley, Deborah A. "Empty 'Text,' Fecund Voice: Self-Reflexivity in Barth's *Lost in the Funhouse.*" *Contemporary Literature* 26 (Winter 1985): 460–81. The political implications of Barth's absorption with language.

INDEX

The index does not include reference to material in the notes.

INDEX

INDEX

INDEX

INDEX

Mundungus (Gus) Turner, 168, 178, 180, 206
Oroonoko Turner, 168
T. Wallace Whittaker, 33
Dr. Welleck, 61

Essays
The Friday Book, 3, 5, 14, 92, 149, 199
"The Literature of Exhaustion," 4, 54, 196
"The Literature of Replenishment: Postmodernist Fiction," 8, 196
"Tales Within Tales Within Tales," 199

Fiction
Chimera, 4, 5, 9, 15, 107, 112, 131–48, 149, 150, 173, 188, 203
  Original ordering, 132
  Use of Mythology, 133–47
  "Dunyazadiad," 131–32, 136, 138, 139, 141, 144
    The issue of telling and listening to stories, 136–40
    The relationship of sex and narration, 140–41
  "Perseid," 131–32, 139
    The relationship of life and stories, 141–44
  "Bellerophoniad," 131, 139, 144–47
    Recounting and altering myth, 144–47
The End of the Road, 3, 24, 50, 52–72, 73, 107, 146, 150, 154, 161
  The nihilism of, 52–62
  The role-playing of Jake Horner, 55–60
  Jake's deceptive use of narration, 62–63
  Joe's existentialism, 64–66
  Rennie's tragic self-effacement, 66–71
The Floating Opera, 3, 6, 24–51, 52, 53, 54, 62, 63, 66, 70, 73, 81, 107, 150, 153, 167, 190
  Publishing information, 24, 26–27
  Paradox in, 25–26
  Existential vision, 25–27
  Various masks of Todd Andrews and Harrison Mack, 35–41

INDEX

INDEX

INDEX

INDEX